By D. James Kennedy

KNOWING THE WHOLE TRUTH

Basic Christianity and what it means in your life

D. JAMES KENNEDY

Fleming H. Revell Company
Old Tappan, New Jersey

Scripture quotations in this volume are from the King James Version.

Permission to quote "The End of the World" from *New And Collected Poems 1917–1976* by Archibald MacLeish is gratefully acknowledged. Copyright © 1976 by Archibald MacLeish. Reprinted by permission of Houghton Mifflin Company.

Library of Congress Cataloging in Publication Data
Kennedy, D. James (Dennis James), 1930–
   Knowing the whole truth.

   1. Apostles' Creed.   I. Title.
BT993.2.K46   1985   238'.11   84-27544
ISBN 0-8007-1407-5

*This book is affectionately dedicated
to the millions of Christians
around the world in hundreds of communions
who, in spite of their differences,
regularly confess their oneness in Christ
as they proclaim their belief
in the Apostles' Creed.*

Contents

THE APOSTLES' CREED

I believe in God the Father almighty,
Maker of heaven and earth, and in
Jesus Christ, his only Son, our Lord,
who was conceived by the Holy Ghost,
born of the Virgin Mary, suffered under
Pontius Pilate, was crucified, dead,
and buried; he descended into hell;
the third day he rose again from the
dead; he ascended into heaven and
sitteth on the right hand of God the
Father almighty; from thence he shall
come to judge the quick and the dead.
I believe in the Holy Ghost, the holy
catholic church, the communion of the
saints, the forgiveness of sins, the
resurrection of the body, and the life
everlasting.

Preface

In our day, when denominational walls have been built so high that many outsiders believe that different denominations are actually different religions, it behooves us to remind ourselves and the world that, in spite of our differences, we have "One Lord, one faith, one baptism," and that we are in fact the one body of our Lord, Jesus Christ.

At a time, also, when unbelief is militant and armed, it is incumbent upon us as Christians to declare unequivocally our faith in the historic tenets of Christianity.

Furthermore, at a time when there is great superficiality of belief and confusion of doctrine, it behooves us as Christians to examine in depth and clarify in our minds and hearts the basic doctrines of our faith.

To that end this book has been written and is sent forth with the prayer that the Lord Jesus Christ, who is the Head of the church, and the object of its faith, would send His Spirit to accompany these words, that faith may be engendered or strengthened in the hearts of many, to the glory of His incomparable name.

D. James Kennedy
Fort Lauderdale, Florida
Fall 1984

KNOWING THE WHOLE TRUTH

CHAPTER 1

The Apostles' Creed Today

"Lord, I believe; help thou mine unbelief."
Mark 9:24

IN THE Apostles' Creed we have the very essence of Christianity. It is a condensation of Christianity, a distillation of the most vital elements of the Christian faith.

In the midst of a century when atheism is rampant and unbelief is everywhere making itself felt, I believe that it is necessary that we once again declare our faith in the great central, basic tenets of the Christian religion. And that Creed is a wonderful thing. It is a marvelous little document. When you examine it carefully, it blazes with color; it radiates romance. And if you really understand what it means, then it sounds like a battle cry or a trumpet blast. It only requires that we wipe away some of the dust of the ages so that we might see the light that scintillates out from those short, sharp, crisp sentences that are known to us all.

It does not argue. It throws down the gauntlet. It is an affirmation, a declaration. It is a manifesto of a Messiah who has come to conquer the world. And, of course, it should never be mumbled or even merely recited. To do it right, it ought to be shouted, asseverated. It ought to begin with a flourish of trumpets—a fanfare with state trumpets would be appropriate, I believe, because upon the great truths that are averred in this magnificent creed men are called to stake their lives. In fact, in various parts of our world today men and women are doing precisely that: They are staking their lives on these truths.

What do you believe? What is really the most significant

thing in your life? What is it that controls your life? Everyone
burns incense to something. Down in the deep crypt of the
subconscience of every man there is an altar upon which he
burns his incense. Everyone gives himself to something. What
is it that really controls your life? Is it wealth? Fame? Pleasure?
Leisure? Are you living for the great triune God?

If the Creed seems dull and dead to you, then either you
ought to change your creed or let your creed change you. And I
hope that, as we consider the great truths of the Creed, as we
polish up the brass to let it gleam again, that these magnificent
truths will grip your mind with something of the freshness they
had when the world first heard them.

Reasons for Discussing the Creed

The Apostles' Creed is a marvelous statement. I have chosen
it, first of all, because of its *universality*. It is something which
virtually every group of Christians everywhere can agree upon.
I do not know of any group of real Christians that could not
recite the Apostles' Creed. And I think that it is important in
this day and time, when atheism is militant and armed, that
Christians let the world know that we are not a bunch of separate sects, but that we hold great truths in common.

As Pascal said: "In essentials, unity; in nonessentials, liberty;
and in all things, charity." That is a great motto to try to follow
in our lives. And in this Creed we are declaring those essentials
which we hold with a unanimity throughout the world.

I have chosen it also because of its *simplicity*. The Athana-
sian or Nicene or Constantinopolitan Creeds are rather complex and are theologically obtuse. But the great cadences of the
Apostles' Creed are simplicity itself and can be understood
even by a child.

I have also chosen it for its *antiquity*. It is the oldest creed
that has come down to the church. Though it was not written
by the Apostles themselves, it has come down to us from the
very earliest centuries of the church. It therefore has an authority that has been verified through the ages.

Need for a Creed

I believe. Now, there are some people who say that they do not really need a creed. They do not have a creed. Well, of course, that is an absurdity since the word *creed* comes from the Latin word *credo,* which means "I believe." If anyone believes anything he has a creed. And since it is not possible for a person to live his life without believing something, then everyone has a creed. Whoever you are, you have a creed. Even the atheist believes in the persistence of protoplasm and matter. He has a creed. He believes in something. The hedonist believes in pleasure. Everyone believes in something; everyone has his creed. But here is the most ancient of Christian creeds—and the most noble of creeds.

Studdert Kennedy said: "You don't really believe your creed until you want to say it standing at spiritual attention with the roll of drums in your ears, the light of love dazzling your eyes, and all the music of a splendid world crashing out a prelude to its truth." How true that is! And I hope that when you say the Apostles' Creed you pour heart and soul into it, so that all who hear you might know that you really *believe* these great and dynamic truths. *I believe in God.* That is the most significant statement that any person could possibly make.

Dr. Mortimer Adler, the editor of the *Great Books of the Western World,* in his chapter on God, says that "all of the writers of all of the great books of the western world are included in this chapter with the exception of just one or two pure mathematicians. Why? Because more consequences flow from belief in or disbelief in God than any other single source."

More consequences come from believing in God or not believing in God. And yet, amazing as it seems, if you turn on television today you would suppose that belief in God is the most totally irrelevant thing imaginable. Tragically, you will not find one Christian portrayed in any continuing TV series about contemporary life in America. If you were a visitor from

Mars you would, no doubt, assume that Christianity became extinct years ago. And yet, the belief in God is the most important belief that anyone could ever have.

Pascal, again, said in his famous wager: "If I bet that there isn't a God and there isn't—nothing gained, nothing lost. But if there is—eternal loss. If I bet that there is a God, and there is, then eternal gain!" Well, you know, we are not betting on God. It is not like flipping a coin to see how it lands, simply choosing heads or tails and maybe having a feeling about it. There is all manner of evidence by many infallible proofs that Christ showed Himself alive from the dead, having been raised by God. And God has demonstrated His presence over and over again.

Only Belief Is Needed

Many people are astounded by the fact that the Bible never attempts to prove God. It doesn't set forth arguments about the existence of God. It no more tries to prove God than you would try to prove the existence of your wife and the children. "The fool hath said in his heart, There is no God" (Psalms 14:1).

The existence of God was so clearly seen and understood by the ancient Jewish people that only a fool could possibly believe that He did not exist. "The heavens declare the glory of God and the firmament showeth His handiwork" (Psalms 19:1).

Napoleon and his army were sailing across the waters of the Mediterranean to Egypt. On the voyage, his generals were gathered one night on the ship's deck and were arguing about God. A number of atheists, one after another, were setting forth their views and their arguments about why they believed that God did not exist. Napoleon had a great mind and no doubt had pondered these ideas himself, but he listened to their arguments patiently. Finally, when they concluded, they looked to him to see his reaction. He simply looked up at the night sky with the millions of stars coruscating in the black heavens above. Waving his hand, he said, "But, monsieur, who made all that?" The heavens declare the glory of God!

God does not need to put a sign up in the heavens saying, "Made by God." It is very obvious that they weren't made in Japan. No one but God could make the heavens. God doesn't have to sign the sunset on the bottom half of the picture because no one but God could paint a sunset. Immanuel Kant, the great philosopher, said that two things amazed him and made him realize that God existed: One was the starry heavens above, and the other was the moral law within—the conscience which God had placed within him. But, the fool still says in his heart that there is no God.

The amazing thing is that the Bible states that only a fool says there is no God. And yet I have never met an atheist who did not believe that he was intellectually superior to every person who ever believed in God. This is in spite of the fact that probably 99 percent of all of the great thinkers who ever lived have strongly believed in God.

Atheists consider themselves to be intellectually above such beliefs. And yet they do not even realize that it is illogical to be an atheist. Atheism is what is known in logic as a universal negative. It is saying that nowhere in the entire universe does such a thing as God exist. It is like saying, "Nowhere in the universe is there such a thing as angels or little green men or heaven or hell or anything else." Now, it is obvious that before one can say he knows that there are no little green men in this universe, he has to have an intimate knowledge of every nook and cranny of the universe. One must be incredibly knowledgeable about all things to know that there are no angels or little green men. Indeed, to know that there is no God, one has to be omniscient. No man is omniscient, only God! Therefore, to know that there is no God, one must needs be God! So, the man is a fool who says that there is no God.

Now there are many arguments for the existence of God. There is the cosmological argument and the teleological argument and the ontological argument and the moral argument.

But there is basically one argument for the denial of God; and that is the immoral argument. "The fool hath said in his heart, There is no God. They are corrupt, they have done abominable works, there is none that doeth good." That is the immoral argument for the nonexistence of God.

I remember the time that Robert Ingersoll, one of the great atheists or skeptics of the early part of this century, was going around the country lecturing against God, against the Bible, against Christianity, and against Christ. He was waxing eloquent about why there was no God, why there was no judgment to come, and why people would never be called to account for their lives. About that time, in the back of the hall, a drunk stood uncertainly to his feet, raised his hand, and said, "You tell 'em, Bobby boy, we're countin' on you." And I think that is the way it is with a lot of immoral people. They are just hoping and praying to God that there is no God. Because if there is, they are going to be called to account for what they have done in their life. *I believe in God.*

The agnostic is one step closer than the atheist. The agnostic says that he does not really know whether there is a God or not. And a lot of people think that is a very sophisticated term, and so they delight in calling themselves agnostics rather than atheists. But, you know, Paul said, "Brethren, I would not have you to be agnostic." Do you remember that text? You may doubt that there is such a statement in Scripture because you are reading it in English and not in Greek. If you were reading it in Greek that is precisely what it says: "Brethren, I would not have you to be *agnostic*" (Romans 1:13). The English says, "Brethren, I would not to have you ignorant"—ignorant and agnostic are exactly the same words. One comes from the Greek and the other from the Latin. *Agnostos,* in Greek, and *ignoramus,* in Latin, both mean the same thing! The agnostic is simply ignorant. He is ignorant of the fact that he has not examined the evidence. He has not used the mind that God has given to examine the evidence.

I have never met an agnostic who ever sat down to read one book on the evidences for the Christian faith, or the existence of God, or the resurrection of Jesus Christ. The agnostics are ignorant of these things. They may be very learned in some other fields, but I have found, over and over again, that when it comes to theology or biblical matters they are incredibly ignorant.

Need to Believe in the Father

"I believe in God, the Father Almighty." Ah, that is a great and glorious sound!

Did you ever hear a young fellow about twelve years old say in talking to another lad about his age, "My father can whip your father any day." Well, that makes him very secure. I remember it wasn't too many years ago that my daughter was quite convinced that I could whip anybody in the world. I remember Muhammad Ali was fighting a fight, and she said to me one time, "You could beat him, couldn't you, Daddy?"

"Sure, Jennifer," I replied. "You know that Daddy can do anything."

The Christian has got to be an optimist because his Father *can* whip their father any day. And who is *their* father? Jesus said, "You are of your father the devil, and his works you do." Yes, we can't possibly be pessimistic, because our Father is almighty; He is the Almighty God, the One who can do all things—the One that stretches forth His hand and there is none that can stay it or say unto Him, "What are you doing?" He is that One who does according to His will among the armies of heaven and the inhabitants of the earth; that One who can say that He will do all of His pleasure, the Almighty, infinite, omnipotent, omniscient, God! That is the One who is *our* Father.

"I believe in God, the Father." What a tremendous revelation that was! Do you realize that no Jew would ever have called God his father? The kings were called the sons of God, but for an average Israelite the idea that God was his father was the farthest thought from his mind. God was the Holy One. "Holy, holy, holy, Lord God Almighty." What is "holy"? It means to be wholly other; to be altogether different; to be

completely separate from sinners; to be transcendent; to be unapproachable.

The Apostles said to Jesus: "Lord, teach us how to pray."
And Jesus said, "Pray this way: 'Our Father. . . .' " What a tremendous revelation! What has become for many people a cli-
ché was an incredible revelation when it was first given by God
through His Son, Jesus Christ. And He went even farther than
that when He said that he would call God "Abba." Abba!
Abba is an Aramaic word, a diminutive of the word Father. It
would literally be translated, "Daddy."

God is spoken of as the "Wholly Other"—transcendent and
unapproachable. Yet who could be more approachable than a
daddy? How natural for a little child to run and throw her
arms around her father's waist saying, "Daddy." That is what
Jesus revealed that God is to us. He is our Father—the infinite,
Almighty, all-powerful One, is our Father. And He loves us
with a Father's love. What greater love could there ever possibly be than the love of a father for us—the Father who so loved
us that He gave His own Son!

Some time ago I was sitting in a home talking to some people about Christ and about their hope of eternal life. *Their*
hope of salvation was based entirely upon the good that they
had done. They recited a long narration of their moralities and
benevolences. They told about how they had gone to church,
had given money, had prayed, and had done this and that and
the other thing.

I pondered how I could make them see what a grievous error
this is. Finally, to make my point, I proposed the following hy-
pothetical, yet relevant, situation.

"Suppose that your door was suddenly broken open and in
rushed six or eight policemen—with guns drawn," I said.
"They threw me on the floor, put my hands behind me,
slapped on handcuffs, and started to take me away. But you
say, 'Wait a minute! What's going on here?' And the police answer: 'This is a notorious criminal. He has killed more than a
dozen people. He has robbed banks. He has kidnapped people.
Why, you're lucky that you got through this evening with your

hide in one piece, having spent time with him alone. Why, he is the number one wanted man in America—public enemy number one.' You say, 'He is? We thought he was a minister!'

" 'Don't let him fool you. He's got more characters he plays than you can imagine.' So they take me away. And you read in the paper about my trial: I am convicted of all of these heinous crimes and am sentenced to die in the electric chair.

"But you're a Christian and you know that Christ said that you should love your neighbor—and I am at least your neighbor. The Bible also says you should love your enemies. So, you decide you ought to do something for me. You go down to the judge and say, 'Judge, we want to help him. He seemed like a nice enough fellow. What can we do?'

"The judge says, 'Nice enough fellow? Why, that man murdered more than a dozen people.' You say, 'Yes, but there must be something that we can do.' After a long pause, one of you says, 'I will give my life for him.'

"The judge says, 'Well, now that's a very touching and noble sentiment. But this man has killed more than a dozen people. I am afraid that would not be an adequate sacrifice. However, do you have a child?' You say, 'Yes, we have one son. He is fifteen.' And the judge says, 'I think that would be an adequate sacrifice.' Ah, no one could do that. 'Greater love hath no man than this, that a man lay down his life for his friends.' But 'God so loved the world he gave his only begotten Son. . . .' Ah, there is a love that is beyond our understanding! You go home. You pray about it. You wrestle with it. You agonize over it.

"Finally the two of you make up your mind. You decide to do it! You bring your son down to the judge and say, 'We are going to do it.' The judge says, 'I am afraid you'll have to do it yourself. You see, no guard could inflict sufficient punishment. (It wasn't a Roman centurion that inflicted an infinite penalty upon Christ; it was the Father Himself. "It pleased the Lord to bruise him; he hath put Him to grief." "We did esteem him stricken, smitten by God and afflicted." [Isaiah 53:10, 4]. So, you must shave his head and you must put the clamps on his ankles and wrists; and you must pull the switch, over and over again until he is dead.'

"So you go through with it: You pull down the switch and you notice the look of complete horror in the eyes of your son. You watch him writhe and die in agony.

"The guards come to my cell to tell me what you have done. They tell me about your son who died in my place and about the love that prompted you to do this thing. They tell me that though I am a no-good, I am, nevertheless, free. I walk out the front gate of the prison.

"A couple of days later, you are seated in a booth in a restaurant. You are not really hungry, but you didn't feel like fixing something, and so you are just sort of stirring your food around on the plate. But suddenly I walk in with a friend and sit down in the booth next to you; I don't see you, though you see me. You hear my friend say to me, 'Kennedy, how in the world did you ever get out? I read in the paper that they were going to cook your goose. What happened?' And I reply, 'Well, you see, that was all a big mistake. They realized when they looked at my record that I was really a pretty decent sort of fellow. They found, in fact, that there were millions of people that I've never killed. There were thousands of banks that I never robbed. In fact, I even put money into one or two. I was a Boy Scout when I was young—helped a couple of old ladies across the street. And I was a pretty decent sort of a fellow. In fact, they thought that I was such a splendid chap that they decided to let me go.'

"All of this time you are seated in the next booth—and you know that the only reason I am walking around alive is because there is a new grave on the other side of town! It was love, love, that motivated you to give up your child for me. It was love that enabled you to pull the switch that he might die for me. But I wonder now, as you listen to my words, how you feel about me now?"

A six-year-old was reciting John 3:16 in Sunday school, but he got it a little bit mixed up. He said, "For God so loved the world, He gave His only *forgotten* Son. . . ." I thought when I heard that, *Ah, that's the religion of most people in America today. God's only forgotten Son! They trust in everything they have done, but they forget all about Christ.* Regardless of what anyone thinks about the death of Jesus Christ on the cross, I can tell you this: To the Father in heaven who gave His son, it's the most important thing in all of the world.

"I believe in God, the Father"—a Father who loved us with an immeasurable love—a love that even gave His Son so that we, who trust in Him, might have forgiveness as a free gift of eternal life if we would rest our souls upon Him.

Someone has well said that when asked, "How much does God love us?", Jesus answered, "This much"—and stretched out His hands, and died.

CHAPTER 2

Maker of Heaven and Earth

"When I consider thy heavens, the work of thy fingers, the moon and the stars, which thou hast ordained; What is man, that thou art mindful of him? and the son of man, that thou visitest him?"

Psalms 8:3, 4

"I BELIEVE in God, the Father Almighty; Maker of heaven and earth." This is a basic and fundamental premise of the Christian religion. Our God is that One who has created this universe.

I remember Dr. Manford Gutzke at Columbia Seminary saying that there is no difficulty believing in such miracles, as, for example, the virgin birth. If we believe in a God who created the vast expanse of the heavens and the myriad of galaxies, then it was a small thing for Him to implant a single cell in the womb of the virgin Mary. The concept of a God of creation lies behind the concept of all other miracles. If we cannot believe in the God who performed the mightiest miracle of all—creating the universe—then belief in all other miracles will evaporate as well.

Yet, today, a strong opposing voice says, in effect, "I do not believe in any God who is the Maker of heaven and earth." And we are told today that intelligent and educated people believe that no one made the heavens and the earth; that they formed themselves and have existed from eternity. Now, that, indeed, is a marvelous thing in itself: We have a creation without a Creator—a making without a Maker!

We are told that the universe began with a big bang. The physicist George Gamow postulated this idea that the universe is expanding and thus began with an initial explosion. But the evolutionists soon realized that this explanation would not do, because an expanding universe obviously implies a beginning—a point in time when everything exploded and began.

The "big bang" theory gave way to an "oscillating universe." We are told that, after the expansion, gravity took over and its power of attraction pulled on the galaxies until they collapsed again and exploded once more. Furthermore, if we go back through history, we would find an oscillating universe—the same process repeating itself over and over again eternally. This, we are told, is the way things really were. Therefore, because there was no beginning, there was no Beginner. The universe is eternal! No Creator is needed!

These theories are interesting because in the last five years virtually every basic tenet of evolution has completely crumbled.

The "Oscillating Universe"

The first of these tenets is the oscillating universe, which was held to be a doctrine of faith. Remember, evolution is a religion—a faith. It is built on the evidence of things not seen, on experiments that will not come off, on intermediate forms that are not found, and on all sorts of other things that just never seem to happen.

There is, in fact, no evidence for the idea of an oscillating universe; it was postulated only because it was necessary to get rid of God. If the universe did not oscillate, there had to be a beginning. And if there was a beginning, everyone from Aristotle on knew that there had to be a First Mover, and that First Mover was God. That could not be allowed! So, the concept of an oscillating universe became the principal dogma of the faith of evolution.

Yet, within the last several years, Drs. Gunn and Sandage of the Hale Observatory and the Mount Palomar Observatory, respectively, after fifteen years of experiments with the "red shift" of the galaxies, came to a startling conclusion. They said that all of the observable data indicate that the universe will never collapse. Ninety percent of the mass necessary for it to collapse gravitationally does not exist, they found, and, therefore, it will expand forever. Ergo, there must have been a beginning! The theory of the oscillating universe has been exploded! And one of the basic tenets of evolution has disappeared.

A Reducing Atmosphere

The second foundational principle of evolution, which also has vanished, is the concept of a reducing atmosphere. Back in 1936 the Russian scientist Oparin postulated that life began as amino acids bound together and formed molecules, and then biopolymers that formed proteins, and these finally got together and formed a living cell. But he knew what all scientists know: This process could not happen in an atmosphere that contained oxygen, because oxygen is absolutely destructive to the preliving biopolymers, preventing their binding and never allowing them to form a cell.

Therefore, scientists postulated an early atmosphere consisting of hydrogen, methane, ammonia, and water vapor—with no free oxygen. There was no evidence for that, but evolution is based upon the evidence of things not seen, because it is a faith—it is a religion in spite of everything that you hear. It is the religion of "no God." Now tests have been made. And it is very interesting, I think, that whenever any facet of evolution has proved testable, the tests have shown evolution to be wrong.

Recently, geologists and other scientists, examining the atmosphere of the planet earth and the three planets closest to earth, and the oldest rocks on earth, have concluded that the earth's early atmosphere was oxygenized. It was an oxygenated atmosphere, not a reducing atmosphere of hydrogen, methane, and ammonia, they say. It was virtually the same atmosphere that we have today—oxygen was present. What does that mean? The molecules and the enzymes could never have formed into proteins and joined together into a cell because the oxygen would have had a deadly effect, preventing that from happening. So, the reducing atmosphere theory has disappeared, and another basic tenet of the god of evolution has fallen on its face like Dagon the fish god before the Ark of the Lord.

Stanley Miller's famous experiment (putting a spark into an atmosphere of methane, hydrogen, and ammonia, and causing some amino acids to bind together) is seen to be irrelevant, though virtually every biology textbook in America has shown that this is the way life began. All of these books, say the authorities, have to be rewritten.

In an article in *Science* magazine, entitled, "Oxygen in the Precambrian Atmosphere," the conclusion is made: Earth had an oxygenic atmosphere! The article states further that some biologists refused to face this fact, due either to prejudice or out-and-out hostility to the facts of science when such facts are hostile to the evolutionary hypothesis.

Now all of these things wherein evolution has destroyed itself have been set forth by evolutionists themselves. We have an enormous revolution taking place within the camp of the evolutionist today. I venture to say that not one supposed fact that you learned in school about evolution is still held by the leaders of that movement today.

Uniformitarianism

A third principle underlying the concept of all evolution was uniformitarianism, the idea that the geology of this earth has always been essentially what it is today, that what changes have occurred in the earth's physical structure have done so uniformly all over the earth throughout history. There was no Noachian flood; there was no catastrophe. Catastrophism went out over a hundred and thirty years ago with the introduction by Lyell of the idea of uniformitarianism. Darwin developed his concept of evolution upon this platform—things pretty well have always continued the way they are; it is just a matter of sedimentation and of erosion; things can be traced back to just about the way they are today; there was no catastrophe, no Noachian flood. But now we find that uniformitarianism has been catastrophized. Indeed, it is now gone!

Stephen Jay Gould, of Harvard, a leading evolutionary proponent in America today, says: "Gradualism (Darwin's idea that by millions of micromutations, species were slowly changed into higher species) . . . was a prejudice of 19th century liberalism facing a world in revolution." What were supposedly the assured results of science were nothing other than theories based upon a liberal prejudice, we are told.

D. V. Ager says, "The fossil record does *not* show gradual evolution, but sudden explosion." Now, who is he? A creationist? No, he is the president of the British Geological Association. I assure you that he is no biblicist or creationist. According to these and many other modern scientists, uniformitarianism, the foundation of Darwinian evolution, has collapsed. Uniformitarianism is out. And catastrophism as the Bible has always taught is back in again.

The Spontaneous Formation of Life

Fourthly, the spontaneous formation of life has been proved impossible. We have been told, for over a century, that amino acids gradually got together and formed protein molecules which bonded together and formed the first cell. Based on what we know of the cell today (Darwin referred to the simple, single cell), the simplest single cell is more complex than anything man has ever created. We need to keep that in mind. Think of the largest computer that man has ever made. The simple, single cell is more complex than that! Some two trillion chemical reactions are taking place in every cell of your body every second of your life. It is the most complex thing imaginable, more complex than New York City's telephone system. Studies of the laws of probability have shown that it would be impossible for a human cell to form spontaneously.

Dr. Francis Crick, credited as the co-discoverer of DNA,* decided to find out what the possibilities were that such an incredibly complex molecule as DNA should be formed sponta-

---

* DNA—deoxyribonucleic acid—"the key substance in the transmission of hereditary characteristics from generation to generation" (*The New Columbia Encyclopedia*)

neously. Under the microscope the DNA molecule appears as a tiny thread in the shape of a complex double helix (spiral), with the various genes arranged on that thread. Dr. Crick concluded that even the supposed four-and-a-half-billion-year history of earth would not have been long enough to produce a single living cell by chance. So he said that life came from some advanced species on some other planet in this or another galaxy, through what he called "directed panspermia": advanced beings sending forth sperm seeds into the universe which finally landed on earth and produced life as we know it. Thus, one of the world's greatest authorities on the living cell says it never could have formed by chance on this earth in spite of everything our children have been taught. His solution, however, only extends the shadow of the problem and raises the question, where did this advanced species come from? This involves us in what is known as an infinite regress.

At about the same time Dr. Crick was postulating this explanation, Sir Frederich Hoyle of Cambridge, one of the world's leading astronomers and mathematicians and the creator of the "steady state" cosmogony, was engaged in mathematical studies with Dr. Chandra Wickramasinghe in England. The object of their study: the possibility of a living cell arising anywhere in the entire cosmos in the supposed twenty-billion-year history of the universe! Their conclusion: There is a zero possibility that by random chance such a thing could happen anywhere in the universe even in twenty billion years! Though they were atheists, they said that the only way that life could ever have come into existence was through the application of an immense intelligence which, they said, "you may wish to call God."

So we see that the spontaneous formation of life is impossible. Sir Hoyle emphasized the conclusion by saying, "The notion that . . . the operating programme of a living cell could be arrived at by chance in a primordial organic soup on this earth is evidently *nonsense of a high order*." Here is one of the greatest living mathematicians and astronomers saying that what you and your children have been learning in school for decades is *nonsense* of the highest order!

Transitional Forms

Fifthly, transitional forms served as the essence of Darwin's theory: Each species moved up or evolved to a different species by thousands and tens of thousands of micromutations and tiny transitional forms. Therefore, there should have been billions of intermediate forms. But now we discover that these transitional forms have disappeared. In fact, they never existed. They are the forever missing links.

Gould of Harvard, and Niles Eldredge, of the American Museum of Natural History, have said that it has long been a trade secret of paleontologists that intermediate forms do not exist. This, in spite of the fact that your children in schools throughout this country are being taught that they do. They are a figment of the imagination of paleontologists. They do not exist! And, therefore, the proponents have had to abandon the concept of missing links and intermediate forms. So we see that all of the foundations of evolution in the last five years have completely crumbled. Therefore, I can say with confidence, "I believe in God, the Father Almighty, Maker of heaven and earth."

The Disastrous Consequences of the Theory of Evolution

Well, what difference does it make where this earth and this world come from? Whether God created it or whether it just evolved? Or whether God used evolution as a way of making it? A lot of people would like to solve the problem with a compromise of that sort. You should remember that though a lot of the followers of evolution have tried to come up with a theistic, evolutionary view, the leaders of evolution have all been atheists or agnostics. You have two views that are contrary to each other, and you must choose between the two.

Sir Julian Huxley, head of UNESCO* (1946–1948), said that

* *United Nations Educational, Scientific, and Cultural Organization.*

God is coming to resemble the fading smile of the Cheshire cat in *Alice's Adventures in Wonderland.* The God of the Gaps, the God needed to fill in the gaps that supposedly were being filled by evolution, is slowly disappearing and becoming totally unnecessary, he said. Anyone who supposes that some compromise is possible is only showing his naiveté, either in understanding the Scripture or understanding evolution itself.

What difference does it make? Well, the consequences of evolution are and have been disastrous! For example: If you believe in evolution then you believe that life has no purpose. One of the main enemies of the evolutionist is teleology or purpose, the idea that there is some goal or purpose for life. To the evolutionist, man's life is simply a matter of random chance—the concatenation of certain amino acids and proteins that came together in the primeval slime and formed you with no foresight of anything in the future—no purpose whatsoever.

If you stepped outside your door this morning and noticed in the corner of the porch that there was a pile of dust and leaves and debris that had been blown there by the wind and the rain during the night, you would never think of asking yourself: "What is the purpose of that pile of dust?" Does it have a purpose? What is it for? Obviously it has no purpose at all because random chance can never produce purpose. Hundreds and hundreds of automobiles surround our church every Sunday. Do they have a purpose? Yes.

Purpose is always created by intelligence, by the application of intelligence to create something for a purpose. Creation is always for a purpose, whereas evolution is purposeless. Therefore, if you would have any purpose for your life you have to abandon any concept of evolution.

No Meaning for Life

The evolutionary hypothesis leaves no meaning or significance for life. You can go to the beach and look at all of the wavy lines produced on the sand by hundreds of millions of waves that have splashed upon the beach, and you will never find any significance or meaning to them. Should you suddenly discover written in the sand the words, "To be or not to be; that is the question," you may be sure that they were not written by the waves, but were written by some intelligence; pure random chance produces no meaning for life at all. That is why Darwin could say that he sometimes wondered if his speech had any more significance than the chattering of monkeys.

The evolutionary view produces no hope. Everything is to be destroyed in the heat death of the universe. Man has no future beyond the mortician's bench or a dark hole in the ground. So all of man's future hopes disappear in the evolutionary miasma.

Furthermore, there is no morality because it is impossible to produce, on an evolutionary basis, any sort of ethical or moral system. You have no morality but the morality of the jungle: the survival of the fittest. (The concept of the survival of the fittest has been embarrassingly discovered to be nothing other than a tautology, a meaningless phrase, since Darwin never defined what the fittest were. You simply have the same thought set forth in the subject and in the predicate. Who are the fittest? They are simply those who survive. So the survival of the fittest means nothing more than the survival of the survivors, which is meaningless again.) Evolution dictates that morality is of man's making (since there is no God); there are no fundamental truths to live by, only biological survival to fight for at all costs.

Whenever evolution has been applied to a modern state you have unmitigated terror and horror. For example, in Nazi Germany, Hitler was a fanatical follower of Nietzsche, who was in turn a disciple of Darwin. Darwin originated the idea of the survival of the fittest races; Nietzsche went on from the survival of the fittest man to the super man; Hitler went from super man to the super race.

Sir Arthur Keith was a leading evolutionist in Britain, the president of the Royal Academy of Science and the author of twenty books defending evolution. He said that what we saw in Nazi Germany was an embarrassment, for in Nazi Germany the principles of evolution were made the policy of a modern technological state. We can see very clearly that the terrors of the holocaust arose out of the writings of Darwin and Nietzsche.

It is well known also that Karl Marx tried to have *Das Kapital* dedicated to Darwin because he looked upon evolution as the expedient which would get rid of God and allow for atheistic communism. Think of the horrors of the "Gulag" where the Soviets, according to Solzhenitsyn, have killed more than sixty million people. The United States Senate committee investigating China concluded that Mao Tse-tung had killed up to sixty-four million Chinese. Communist Russia and China account for a total of one hundred and twenty-four million murders, not to mention Cambodia, Viet Nam, Afghanistan, Africa, Latin America, and other parts of the world. More people have died under evolutionary, atheistic communism than have died in all of the wars of history.

Furthermore, there is no salvation in the evolutionary process. *The American Atheist* magazine recently said that unless there is a belief in a Fall, there is no need for a Redeemer to undo the effects of the Fall. The only fall that man has experienced, they say, is a fall up the stairs of the evolutionary ladder. And so, Christ becomes a useless excrescence, someone who is unnecessary because there is no need for salvation . . . because there is no original sin . . . for there was no Adam.

Creation is Glorious!

The implications of creation, however, are glorious—quite contrary to the implications of evolution which allows no purpose or meaning, significance, hope or salvation for man. The fact that God is the Maker of heaven and earth means that He is the sovereign Lord of what He has created and that His will will be done on this planet.

Secondly, it means that He is the source of all law and morality. If God has created the world, if He has created us, then He can tell us how we are to live. Therefore, all efforts of human beings to try to erect their own ethics, their own morality, their own laws, apart from what God's Word says, are completely fallacious.

Thirdly, He is the Redeemer of men. Since man has been created perfect and has fallen into depravity and sin, he desperately needs a redeemer. And God, who is the Maker of heaven and earth, has Himself, in the person of His Son, come into the world to redeem mankind.

Fourthly, He holds the future of the world in His hands. And it is a glorious future. God didn't make any *Titanic* destined for disaster. He made the world; He sovereignly controls the world; He has redeemed the world, and He will bring it to its own glorious conclusion. Therefore, the Christian cannot be pessimistic, either about the world itself or about his own future. He can know that Christ will bring him forth out of the grave into an everlasting paradise—if he trusts in Him.

We know that the God who created the world is the God who will call the world into judgment. Of course, this is what has sent the unbelievers fleeing and scurrying into the camp of evolution, *for the simple expedient of getting rid of God.* I heard Julian Huxley himself say once on television that he supposed that the reason why *The Origin of the Species* was welcomed so enthusiastically was because the idea of God interferes with our sexual mores. That is, by accepting Darwin's theory we took the lid off all sorts of sexual permissiveness and perversion. The idea of God interfered with what man really wanted to do, so God was jettisoned. Sin could then prevail.

God, however, is not so easily done away with! He is not the smiling and fading Cheshire cat. No. I am afraid that these unbelievers will find—at the end—the frowning face of an aggrieved God whom they have blasphemed and denied and who will bring them into a real judgment in a real universe. God is the Maker of heaven and earth. And, thank God, He is also the remaker of those of us who will come to Him. If you believe that He has created the world, He can create you anew. He can make you over again into the image of His Son, if you will only come to Christ and place your trust in Him—repenting of your sins, accepting His proffered mercy, the free gift of eternal life which He so graciously extends to us. You can know His forgiveness. You can know His redemption. You can be remade as a new creature in Jesus Christ. Old things will pass away and all things will become new. And you will know from the very depths of your soul that you believe in God, THE MAKER OF HEAVEN AND EARTH, who has remade your soul.

CHAPTER 3

Jesus Christ Our Lord

"For unto us a child is born, unto us a son is given: and the government shall be upon his shoulder: and his name shall be called Wonderful, Counsellor, The mighty God, The everlasting Father, The Prince of Peace."

Isaiah 9:6

"I BELIEVE in God, the Father Almighty, Maker of heaven and earth, and in Jesus Christ." Did you ever think about how the very human name of Jesus is placed in immediate juxtaposition and apparent equality with the name of God, the Father Almighty, Maker of heaven and earth?

Now either there is contained here a great truth or the ultimate blasphemy! Jesus is set forth in the midst of His peers. On the one hand there is the Father Almighty, and on the other there is the Holy Spirit. And the center gem of the diadem is Jesus Christ.

In fact, you may have noticed that the Apostles' Creed says more about Jesus than it says about all else combined. To be completely accurate, the Apostles' Creed says almost twice as much about Christ as it does about everything else combined. The reason is obvious: This is a Christian church, and the great central confession of the Christian church is that Jesus Christ is God come in the flesh.

Do you believe that? Is that the faith which you hold?

The Glorious Attributes of Jesus

This absolutely astonishing person has a very human name. Jesus. That is the name by which He was known to His child-

hood friends, and the name by which He was known in Nazareth, Galilee, and Jerusalem. He was Jesus of Nazareth, or, as
it would have been said in Hebrew, *Joshua,* or *Yoshua.*

That in itself is a marvel! The angel declared, "thou shalt call
his name Jesus; for he shall save his people from their sins"
(Matthew 1:21). You may have never seen the wonder contained in that verse because perhaps you have never thought
about what His name meant or means. The name Yoshua, Joshua, or Jesus means "Jehovah saves." Now take that truth and
place it back into the context and note what you have: "You
shall call His name Jesus [that is, you shall call His name 'Jehovah Saves'], for he will save His people from their sins."

Fully God, Yet Fully Man

The great confession of the Christian church is that Jesus of
Nazareth is Jehovah of hosts. He is the second person of the
triune God—Father, Son, and Holy Spirit. *Fully God!* And yet,
fully man!

When we confess that we believe in Jesus, we are confessing
that we believe that He was, first of all, a man, and that He was
fully a man. Not many people today deny that. In the early
centuries of the church, the Docetists said that Jesus only
seemed to be a man—that he was actually a phantasm and was
not a man at all. But few today would make such a claim. Most
are willing to concede to Him His humanity, while perhaps at-
tempting to deny His deity.

But He was fully human in every way. His ancestry was obviously human: He was born of the virgin Mary; He was of the
seed of David; He was even the descendant of Adam, we are
told by Luke. Furthermore, He had brothers and sisters, according to the Gospel. So, He had a very human ancestry, at
least on His mother's side.

He also had a very human appearance. There was nothing
about Him that caused anyone to think that He was anything
different than a man. "The veil that Godhead wore; shut out
more glory than we could bear." But he was taken to be a man
by His disciples and by His enemies as well. "Is this not the

carpenter's son?" they asked in derision. He was thought to be a man even after His resurrection. Mary mistook Him for the gardener. The disciples on the road to Emmaus thought that He was just any citizen who perhaps was ignorant of the great events which had just transpired in their community. He appeared to be a man; He claimed to be a man; He claimed to be the Son of Man, with an ancestry that reached all the way back to the first man.

He claimed to have a body and a spirit and a soul. And so He did. He experienced all of those things which we, as humans, experience. He hungered and He thirsted. He wept, He slept and He was weary. He was tempted in all ways such as we are. Yet without sin! He suffered and, finally, like us, He died. He was the very human Jesus. But He was also the very perfect Jesus. He had our human nature in all ways, yet He was without sin.

How many times I have heard people say, when having committed some sin, "Well, after all, I am only human," as if humanity and sinfulness were to be equated and were one and the same thing. But I would remind you that when humanity was first created it was without sin. And the time will come, not long hence, I am sure, when we shall be in paradise. There we shall be fully human, but we shall again be without sin. Jesus was perfect humanity. He never sinned. He always did those things which were according to the law of God. He was a perfect human being. He was Jesus. And I believe in Jesus; but not merely Jesus—Jesus Christ. *Christ,* the Greek word for *Messiah,* means "the anointed one." Even as in the Old Testament, the prophets and priests were anointed, the kings were also anointed. So Jesus is the anointed prophet, priest, and king, the Divine Redeemer, the Messiah of God. And the name of Christ points to His deity and reminds us that Jesus was not merely human, but He was also divine. He was the God-man—not a man that became God, but God that became flesh and dwelt among us. He was the *theanthropos,* the God-man.

If He were not God He could be no redeemer. The Scripture

makes it plain that no man can redeem his brother. And the suffering of Christ would not have been sufficient to pay for the sins of the world were they not infinite in value because of the fact that He was divine. No. He was the great Divine Redeemer. All of the big guns of the skeptics and atheists have been aimed at this down through the centuries; all of the unbelievers have denied it. Every one of the cults today denies the unique deity of Jesus Christ—whether Jehovah's Witnesses or the Mormons or Christian Science or all of the modern cults—they all deny the basic foundational tenet of the Christian faith, the Gibraltar upon which all of Christianity stands, that Jesus Christ is the unique God-man come in the flesh.

Omnipotent, Omniscient, Omnipresent

The Bible makes it clear that He exercises the attributes of deity; He has the attribute of *omnipotence*. He Himself declared: "All power is given unto me in heaven and in earth" (Matthew 28:18). And He not only claimed it; He demonstrated it very frequently during His lifetime. He demonstrated His power over nature. He stilled the winds and silenced the waves. He walked upon the sea. He demonstrated His power, His omnipotent power, over the demons, saying, "Get ye hence." And at His command they left in obedience. He demonstrated His power over the very angels of heaven, frequently referring to them, in the most amazing and often overlooked way, as *His* angels. Can you imagine anyone claiming that the vast legions of the angels of God were His own—angels He could command at anytime to do His bidding? In demonstrating His power over disease, all manner of disease fled before His touch. And last, He demonstrated His power even over death. Having raised others in His lifetime, He at last was raised by God's own omnipotent power, thus demonstrating the divine attribute of *omnipotence*.

He also demonstrated the attribute of *omniscience*. John tells us that He revealed Himself or committed Himself unto no man, for He knew what was in all men.

And He also demonstrated the attribute of *omnipresence*. The final thing that Jesus said in the Gospel of Matthew (after having declared the great commission: Go into all the world and preach the gospel) was, "And lo, I am with you always" (Matthew 28:20). And so they went, first by the dozens and scores, and then by the hundreds, the thousands, and the tens of thousands. They have gone and are going into every continent, to every nation and tribe, telling of Jesus in hundreds of tongues and languages. They have crossed the hottest deserts, plunged through the thickest jungles and scaled the highest mountains. And wherever they have gone, on land or sea, always Jesus was with them as He is with us because He is the omnipresent God who is everywhere.

Acts of Deity

Even the great and principal acts of deity are attributed to Christ in the Scripture. We see that the Bible says that He is the Creator. "All things were made by him; and without him was not anything made that was made," says John (John 1:3). He is the Creator of the galaxies. Unto Him is attributed the power of resurrection: He gives life to whom He will and at His voice the dead will come to life and rise out of the graves. To Him is attributed not only the act of resurrection, but also judgment as well. It is Christ who will judge the dead. All judgment has been committed into the hands of the Son that He may be equal with the Father, we are told in John 5:22, 23. Christ will judge the living and the dead. He is God!

Accepted the Worship of Others

It is also, I think, worthy of our note to remember that Jesus accepted the worship of others. How different He is from all other men. Dr. J. Oswald Sanders points out the fact that Jesus stands in marked contrast from all human beings. Do you remember that Jesus often was worshiped? "There came a leper and worshiped him . . ." (Matthew 8:2). "There came a certain ruler, and worshiped him . . ." (Matthew 9:18). The man born blind who was healed by Christ said, "Lord, I believe. And he worshiped him" (John 9:38). Everywhere we read that people worshiped him.

The Pharisees told Jesus to rebuke His disciples so that they would cease to praise and worship His name, and He responded: "If these should hold their peace, the stones would immediately cry out" (Luke 19:40). He received the worship of men. When Thomas looked up into His face and said, "My Lord and my God," He blessed him (see John 20:28); however, John fell upon his knees before an angel, and the angel said, "See thou do it not; for I am thy fellow servant . . . Worship God" (Revelation 22:9).

To worship anything other than the living God is, by definition, idolatry. Therefore, if Jesus were not the living God in human flesh, then He was certainly guilty of accepting the idolatrous worship of many. But He is the living God, different from all others who have lived upon this earth.

The Sinless One

Christ says that all men are sinners, that the heart is deceitful. He says, "For from within, out of the heart of men, proceed evil thoughts . . ." (Mark 7:21). Yet He can say at the same time, "Which of you convinceth me of sin?" (John 8:46). And He has always been the sinless One, the peerless Christ.

Oh, what amiss may I forgive in Thee,
Jesus, good Paragon, thou Crystal Christ.

Jesus was aware of no sin at all, whereas the greatest of saints have been keenly aware of their own depravity. Job moaned about the fact that he had heard of God with the hearing of the ear, but when he saw Him, he said that he lamented in sackcloth and ashes. Or we see Peter saying, "Depart from me; for I am a sinful man, O Lord" (Luke 5:8). And Paul declared that he was "chief" of sinners (see 1 Timothy 1:15). Yet Jesus was aware of no sin whatsoever. The greatest and holiest of all was cognizant of no sin in His life.

Jesus taught His disciples that when they had done all He

had commanded, that they should say of themselves, "We are but unprofitable servants." Is that what He said of Himself? He said, "I do always those things that please" the Father (*see* John 8:29). On the cross, He sought forgiveness for His enemies but sought none for Himself. And in this, even the thief beside Him agreed, saying, "We receive the due reward of our deeds. But this man hath done nothing amiss" (Luke 23:41).

He Has the Ultimate Authority

Jesus teaches us in His Word that in many counselors there is wisdom, and yet Jesus sought the counsel of none. When advice was proffered to Him, He spurned it immediately: "Woman, what have I to do with thee?" (John 2:4). Jesus never sought the advice of the learned or the wise, but He taught as One having the ultimate authority. His word was the final authority in all things, and He placed it over all other authorities. All that came before Him were thieves and robbers. Even about the Old Testament He said, "Moses hath said . . . but *I* say unto you. . . . Ye have heard it hath been said . . . but I say unto you. . . ." And His "Verily, I say unto you . . ." was the ultimate word that could be spoken on any subject. When He completed His Sermon on the Mount, His disciples were astonished. (The Greek text says they were "knocked out" because He taught them, not as the scribes and the Pharisees, but as one having authority.) Jesus gathered all of the world under His personal rule. He said that the highest motive of virtue is to do what you do for "My sake." "For My sake," He said! Can you imagine any preacher who would say, "all that you do in your life, you should do for my sake"? You would suppose him to be mad—an egomaniac. Yet Jesus taught this so naturally that we do not even think about it as we read the Scriptures.

The Apostle Paul said, "We preach not ourselves." Yet, *mirabile dictu,* Jesus preached about Himself. Though He could say that He was meek and lowly of heart, the central theme of His preaching was Himself.

What would you think if you had a preacher who, every Lord's day, stood up and preached about himself? You would soon, I am sure, get another preacher. Yet Jesus did this persistently and consistently.

> I am the way, the truth, and the life. . . .
> I am the door of the sheep. All that ever came
> before me are thieves and robbers. . . .
> I am the good shepherd; the good shepherd giveth
> his life for the sheep.
> I am the vine . . . without me ye can do nothing.
> I am the door; by me if any man enter in, he
> shall be saved. . . .
>
> John 14:6; 10:7, 8, 11; 15:5; 10:9

And so it goes throughout all of His ministry—Jesus Christ preached Himself. He would, indeed, be an egomaniac were He not the incarnate God.

Not A "Good Man"

Jesus was not a good man. He did not allow people that option. When someone came and said, "Good sir," He said, "Stop right there. Why do you call me good? There is none good but One, and that is God" (*see* Luke 18:19). And he hung the man up on the horns of a dilemma: The man was made to realize, even as all others must realize, that either Jesus is God or He is not good.

Christ had already taught that all men are sinful; so if Christ were merely a man, then He is not good. He is either the good God or He is a sinful man. Therefore, it will not do to say, "Oh, Jesus was a wonderful man." No, He was and is the incarnate God; the Creator of the heavens and the earth; the Divine Redeemer; the One who could say, "Before Abraham was, I am" (John 8:58); and take upon His lips the word, *Jehovah,* "I am." Jesus, the human name and Christ, the divine gathering together into the *theanthropos,* the God-man.

The Father's Only Son

I believe in Jesus Christ, His only Son. His *only* Son! Are not we also the sons and daughters of God? Does it not say that those that believe on His name are given power to become the sons of God? Are we not adopted into His family whereby we cry, "Abba, Father"? Yes, we are the adopted sons of God. But Jesus is unique—separate and distinct from all others. He is the essential and natural and eternal and only begotten Son of God. Jesus is forever the Son of God, of the same nature with the Father, eternally—"eternally begotten," said the fathers of the church.

Eternally begotten! What does that mean? I think the best analogy is to consider the sun. We know that the sun produces light; as long as the sun has existed, the sun has produced light. We cannot even imagine the sun existing without producing light. And so it is with God. As long as God the Father has existed, He has eternally begotten the Son. And since God has *always* existed, the Son has eternally been begotten by the Father as His only and eternally begotten Son. The Unique One. The altogether Lovely One who stands apart from all others who have ever lived.

Four Different Pictures Show Only One Character

The four Gospels present four rather different pictures of Christ from different perspectives, backgrounds, and events chosen. Yet, as we read those Gospels, we note that one character seems to rise up from the pages—a character who was unique and altogether lovely.

We begin to see a face. We begin to hear a voice, a voice that speaks with music and poetry that has never been heard before. "Come unto me, all ye that labor and are heavy laden, and I will give you rest" (for your souls) (Matthew 11:28).

And that voice rings down through the centuries. Oh, the skeptics have come with their spectacles, scissors, and paste; and they have cut up the Gospels and pasted them back together again any way they wanted; *Yet, that character still stands and the voice is still heard!* The invitation still comes, and the music still sounds.

Yes, there have been antagonists all right. Nietzsche condemned Christ. He mocked His humility and he dubbed Him a slave. And Nietzsche died in a madhouse! Yet the voice is still heard. Hitler declared of himself that he was a pure pagan and that he would uproot Christianity from the earth. But he ended a charred cinder! The voice is still heard.

And so it is that Christ, by His insistent silence, criticizes His critics and somehow becomes the Final Judge of all of His judges. And that voice is still heard today: "Come unto me, all ye that labor and are heavy laden, and I will give you rest."

Our Lord

He is Jesus Christ, His only Son, our Lord. He is Jesus, the Christ, His only Son but *our* Lord. God hath made Him both Lord and Christ. "Jesus, whom ye have crucified, [is] both Lord and Christ," said Peter (Acts 2:36).

The term *in Christ* describes that aspect of Christ in which He stands before God as the one who reconciles us unto the Father by His divine Messiahship. The term *Lord* has to do with His position over us as ruler and controller of our lives here below.

Is Jesus Christ *your* Lord? Is He *kurios christos,* the Lord Christ? The ruler of *your* heart? There are those who vainly imagine that Jesus somehow may be our Savior without being our Lord. Nothing could be further from the teachings of Scripture. The Word is clear and explicit: "Believe on the *Lord* Jesus Christ, and thou shalt be saved." The earliest confession of the Christian church, the first confession of the Christian church, was very simply this: *Jesus is Lord!* Is He the Lord of *your* life?

In order to be saved, it is essential that we receive Him as Savior and trust in His atoning work; but more than that is necessary. We must understand what He has done for us on the cross. Our hearts must go out to Him saying, "It is the voice of my beloved. I will rise and go unto Him." In addition and of utmost importance, our will must be yielded to Him. Christ must take His place upon the throne of our heart, and He must be Lord of all—or He will not be Lord at all.

I would ask you today: Have you surrendered yourself to the Lordship of Christ?

Have you surrendered your mind to Him? Your energy to Him? Your emotions to Him? Your business to Him? Your family to Him? Your hours and weeks and months and years to Him? Your possessions to Him? Your ambitions to Him? Your hopes to Him?

Is Christ the Lord and Master and King of your life? He will not be Lord at all if He cannot be Lord of all.

A modern Jew said: "The significant fact is that time has not faded the vividness of his image. Poetry still sings his praise. No Muslim ever sings, 'Muhammad, lover of my soul,' nor does any Jew say of Moses the teacher, 'I need thee every hour.' " No! Jesus alone is the lover of our soul—the One whom we need every hour as Savior and Lord and Master of our lives. Oh, that you would learn even now to bow the knee and confess Him as your all-in-all, the King of your heart and soul, and sing with the hymnist:

> All hail the pow'r of Jesus' name!
> Let angels prostrate fall;
> Bring forth the royal diadem,
> And crown Him, crown Him, crown Him—
>   Lord of all!"

CHAPTER 4

The Virgin Birth

*"Therefore the Lord himself shall give you a sign;
Behold, a virgin shall conceive, and bear a son, and
shall call his name Immanuel."*

Isaiah 7:14

A YOUNG minister, freshly minted from theological seminary,
had just taken a pastorate in a rural area peopled by Scandi-
navian folk. One day he decided to invite an old skeptical
farmer, who was something of a curmudgeon, to join him for
church. The man ordinarily did not attend. So he picked him
up and drove him to the service, during which hour he
preached on the subject of the virgin birth. On the way home,
in the car, he asked the old farmer what he thought of the message, to which the man said: "Now, son, if you were to hear that
some young girl got herself pregnant, had a child, and they told
you that it was a virgin birth, would you believe that today?"
(Well, how about it? Would you?) Our minister thought for
a while and then replied, "I would if she lived a life like Jesus'."

You see, science requires that every effect have an adequate
cause. And Jesus Christ, according to the nearly unanimous
testimony of history, lived a peerless and sinless life in the
midst of a universally sinful humanity. Let's now examine the
cause of that life which was lived by one who could say,
"Which of you convinceth me of sin?" And let's further examine that One who was tempted in all ways such as we are, yet
was without sin. There must be some adequate cause for that
life.

The Scripture says that the cause is to be found in His miraculous virgin birth. As the Apostles' Creed declares: "He was conceived by the Holy Ghost; and born of the virgin Mary." Well, modernity, with all of its sophistication and skepticism, has agreed that the virgin birth is too hard to swallow. And liberal and radical theologians, from Harry Emerson Fosdick on down, have agreed in saying that it never happened. Fosdick, the modern popularizer of liberalism some decades ago, said, "I certainly don't believe in the virgin birth and I hope that you don't either." And in many another church in this country, ministers of the modern design have declared unequivocally, as if it were the assured results of modern scientific inquiry, that Jesus was not born of a virgin.

What the Scriptures Say

Well, what shall we say? First, let us ask the question: Does the Scripture indeed teach that He was born of a virgin? Some people are not really clear on that. But of that question and fact there can be no doubt! Both in the Old and the New Testaments the teaching is unequivocal. In fact, the very first promise that God gave of the gospel concerns the virgin birth. It is found in Genesis 3:15. Speaking to the serpent, God said: "I will put enmity between thee and the woman and between thy seed and her seed; it shall bruise thy head, and thou shalt bruise his heel." This is known as the *Protoevangelium,* the first evangel or the first gospel. It was the first promise of God that He would send a Redeemer. The Redeemer was to be the seed of a woman (not of a man, implying a virgin birth) who would bruise the head of and destroy the serpent who brought the curse upon the earth. As the final result, the serpent himself would endure a mortal wound. The *Protoevangelium* was something which was to have an enormous effect upon the whole world. (But I will return to that story in a while.)

Further on in the Old Testament, we see that this is even more clearly spelled out. In Isaiah 7:14 we read: "Therefore the Lord himself shall give you a sign; Behold, a virgin shall conceive, and bear a son and shall call his name Immanuel." That is the same verse Matthew chose to quote in his Gospel.

Nothing could be more clear. We read: ". . . before they came together, she was found with child of the Holy Ghost" (Matthew 1:18). And in verse 20, ". . . for that which is conceived in her is of the Holy Ghost."

It is interesting to note that both Matthew and Luke are the two who teach the doctrine of the virgin birth and give the genealogy of Christ. Therefore, they see no conflict between His genealogy and His miraculous conception. In fact, they go out of their way to make sure everyone understands that there is a distinct difference between the way that Christ was born and the birth of all of His progenitors.

We read, for example, in Matthew that Abraham begat, David begat, Jacob begat, on up to the fact that another Jacob finally begat "Joseph, the husband of Mary, of whom [feminine] was born Jesus, who is called Christ" (1:16). We read that this man begat that man, that man begat that man who begat this person. . . . But Joseph did not beget Christ; rather, Joseph was merely the husband of Mary of whom Jesus was born.

Luke says of Jesus that when He reached thirty years of age, "being (as was supposed) the son of Joseph . . ." (Luke 3:23). So both Matthew and Luke go out of their way to make absolutely clear that Jesus was not Joseph's son.

Mary, when she heard the announcement of the angel Gabriel that she should conceive and bear a child, said, "How shall this be, seeing I know not a man?" And the angel replied, "The Holy Ghost shall come upon thee, and the power of the highest shall overshadow thee; therefore also that holy thing which shall be born of thee shall be called the Son of God" (Luke 1:34, 35). The Scripture makes it abundantly clear that Christ was born of a virgin and conceived by the Holy Ghost.

The Virgin Birth *Does* Make a Difference

But many liberals say that it really doesn't matter: "We don't want to burden the modern mind with such an antiquated idea. It really doesn't make a difference." One day, I decided to consider how much of a difference it does make, and I wrote out the following: If Jesus were not born of a virgin . . .

1. The New Testament narratives are proved untrue and unreliable.
2. Mary is stained with the sin of unchastity.
3. Jesus was mistaken about His paternity.
4. Christ was not born of "the seed of the woman" and is not the fulfillment of the ancient *Protoevangelium.*
5. Jesus was therefore an illegitimate child.
6. He is consequently then not the God-man or Son of God.
7. He was then a sinner like the rest of us.
8. As a sinner he is not the Divine Redeemer.
9. We have then no savior at all.
10. We are yet in our sins and without forgiveness.
11. We have no hope after death.
12. There is no mediator between God and man.
13. If there is no Second Person, there is no Trinity.
14. Christ should have prayed, "Father, forgive us"—not "forgive them."
15. If this miracle is denied, then why not deny them all? Where, indeed, shall we draw the line?

Does it make any difference? It makes all the difference in this world and in the world to come. In fact, it totally subverts the entire Christian gospel and destroys the whole meaning of Jesus Christ as the Divine Redeemer. It robs us of all hope of salvation—*if* Jesus was not virgin-born.

Why then do people not believe it, if it is so important? Basically there are three reasons. First, there are those who deny it because they deny all miracles. They would say that the only reason people believed back then is that they were ignorant of the scientific method. They weren't as knowledgeable as we are about natural laws, and, being ignorant of natural law, they were ignorant of those things which were breaches of natural laws. They supposed all sorts of things to be miracles which really were not.

Was it really because they were simply ancient ignoramuses who believed in miracles? Well, let's look at the facts: Obviously, Joseph was not as acquainted with the scientific method as we are. The average gynecologist today knows a great deal more about conception and childbirth than Joseph ever dreamed.

But Joseph was not born yesterday. He was no fool! When he discovered that Mary was pregnant, he did not say, "Oh, it's probably a virgin birth. No doubt it's the Holy Spirit who has done this thing. Being such an ignorant old fool, I certainly don't believe that she slept with anyone else."

That is not what he said at all! He determined to put her away, to divorce her, having concluded that she was unchaste. It took the visitation of the angel Gabriel to convince him that what was born in her was of the Holy Ghost. Though there were many things they didn't know, they did know about the birds and the bees even back then!

As Dr. Gutzke used to say, if we can believe in a God of creation—a God who has flung from His fingertips the myriad of galaxies which cascade with light across the black sky—it is no great thing to believe that same mighty, omnipotent God could cause a tiny seed to be placed in the womb of a young woman. The fact of the matter is that if we cannot believe in such a tiny miracle as that, then how can we believe in any miracle at all? We probably don't believe that there is a Creator. And if we believe that there is no Creator, we don't even believe in God. Such a person as this needs to be approached from some other point than the virgin birth. I would take that person to the great bastion of truth, the resurrection of Christ, and begin there.

The Argument from Silence

The second reason of those who do not accept some miracles would be the claim that the Gospels of Mark and John say nothing about it and Paul never alludes to it in his epistles.

Dr. Harry Rimmer, now deceased, a Presbyterian minister who held doctorates both in theology and science, once had quite an encounter on the floor of presbytery with a rather radical Presbyterian minister.

A young man being examined for the ministry had proclaimed that he did not believe in the virgin birth. When some of the other ministers began to question him rather severely, an older minister stood up and said that he hoped that they would not make a big point of this because, after all, he said, "I don't believe in the virgin birth either."

Someone asked, "Why not?" And he said, "Well, that should be obvious. It is only mentioned in two places in the New Testament, in Matthew and Luke. Mark knows nothing about it. John never mentions it. And in all of his Epistles, Paul never says one word about it."

Dr. Rimmer rose to his feet and said, "Well, then, just what do you preach for a gospel?"

The minister replied, "I preach the Sermon on the Mount. That's all the gospel anybody needs."

Dr. Rimmer answered that it was not enough for him and then the man asked, "Why not?" Rimmer said, "Because I don't believe it." That came as something of a bombshell in the midst of the presbytery meeting.

"I don't believe that Jesus ever preached the Sermon on the Mount," Rimmer added. The older man again asked, "Why ever not?" The reply was, "It should be very plain to all. Only Matthew and Luke say anything about the Sermon on the Mount. Mark never says one word about it—apparently he never even knew that it had been preached. John never alludes to it at all. And in all of his epistles, Paul never once refers to a Sermon on the Mount. So, obviously, Jesus never preached such a sermon!"

Well, as you can well imagine the old man was rather taken aback. But, indeed, why should we believe that Jesus preached the Sermon on the Mount when it is only told to us by Matthew and Luke, who happened to be the same ones who have told us about the virgin birth?

This is what is known as the argument from silence. And the argument from silence is next to no argument at all. It is the worst of all possible arguments. With it you can prove or disprove almost anything. For example: It is true that Mark never mentions the virgin birth of Christ. It is also true that Mark never mentions the birth of Christ. Therefore, obviously Mark didn't believe that Jesus had ever been born at all in any way! Isn't logic wonderful!

Paul never mentions the virgin birth, though he does refer to the fact that Jesus was "born of a woman, born under the law." But it is also true that Paul never mentioned any of the miracles of Jesus. So, according to the argument from silence, Paul believed that Jesus never worked a miracle at all. And since Paul never mentioned them, obviously they never happened. Therefore, Jesus worked no miracles in His lifetime. And if that is not enough, we might also say that Paul never mentions any of the parables of Jesus. So, quite evidently, Christ never preached any. And that is where the argument from silence leads us.

The Appeal to Pagans

The third argument is the appeal to the pagans by the similarity of heathen legends. It has long been known that there are many supposed "virgin births" or other miraculous births that were supposed to have taken place in the various legends and mythologies of the world. For example, just to name a few: Zeus, the Greek god, came into Alcmene and produced Hercules. Vishnu, in his eighth incarnation or avatar, came out as the virgin-born Krishna. Buddha is supposed to have been virgin-born of his mother, Maya. Augustus Caesar claimed to have had a miraculous birth. And Alexander the Great also claimed to have been miraculously born.

The first thing that we want to realize is that for every original there are also counterfeits. We then must notice the discrepancies and differences that exist. In all the Greek legends of gods and mortals cohabitating, the gods are lusting after some fair mortal woman, for the gods were simply men writ large, with all of the sins and foibles of men, except mortality! In the case of Zeus and Hercules there is deception, lust, and adultery—a far cry from the chaste and holy picture of the virgin birth found in Scripture. In the case of Vishnu, he was supposedly first incarnated as a fish, then a turtle, then a boar, and then a lion; then all sorts of bizarre wonders took place in the birth of Krishna. The mother of Buddha tells the story of a white, six-tusked elephant with blood-red veins that came into her side and brought about the conception of Buddha. Augustus Caesar said that he would have it known that he was born due to the cohabitation of his mother with a serpent. In the case of Alexander the Great, a serpent was found in the bed with his mother, Olympias. A long cry from the Gospels of Luke or Matthew!

But more must be asked, as we consider these and many other cases: Is there some cause for these various stories of a virgin birth?

I would take you back to that which antedates all of them: the *Protoevangelium* referred to before—the promise made to our original parents while still in the garden of Eden. Immediately after the account of the Fall, we read of "the seed of the woman," a unique term which does not appear any other time in Scripture. Elsewhere it is "the seed of a man," but here (in Genesis 3:15) is this unique individual who is to be born of a woman, who is to crush the head of the serpent and endure a mortal wound in so doing. Now this promise of a coming deliverer, who will remove the curse of the world brought on by the serpent, was carried by our early fathers into all parts of the world wherever they went. Students of history know this.

We find that immediately after the flood, a grandson of Noah, Cush, was responsible for building the tower of Babel. This Cush had a son named Nimrod, the mighty hunter, who hunted not only animals but also men. Warfare was Nimrod's primary contribution to the world. He was the first to go to war against his neighbors. He conquered all of Babylonia and Assyria, and went all the way down through Egypt and into Libya. Scholars have traced the rise of all sorts of heathen mythology from this Babylonian source, which came immediately from the grandson of Ham after the flood.

Cush is known by various names: He is *Chaos,* the god of confusion (recall the confusion of tongues at Babel). He is *Merodach,* the great rebel who revolted against God in building the tower. He is *Janus,* whose symbol is the club by which the world was scattered. He is *Hephaistos.* He is also *Vulcan,* with his hammer, who in the same way scattered the children of man across the world. He is *Bel,* the confounder of tongues. He is *Hermes,* which literally means "the son of Ham." He is also *Mercury.*

We see that this original myth began with Cush and with his son Nimrod, who was, according to legend, married to Semiramas, and who was the great hero and first king of Babylon. After his death, his wife Semiramas had him deified and it was then claimed that he was the seed of the woman, that he was virgin-born.

This early Babylonian myth is carried over into Egypt, as is made very clear by the noted Assyriologist, Layard, who discovered Nineveh and examined the Babylonian cylinders and monuments. Layard said that the zodiacal signs . . . show unequivocally that the Greeks derived their notions and arrangements of the zodiac (and consequently their mythology that was intertwined with it) from the Chaldees. The identity of Nimrod with the constellation Orion is not to be rejected. Nimrod, the great hunter. Orion, the great hunter. And so this early rebellion against the worship of the true God and Nimrod's claim to be virgin-born passed over into Egyptian mythology.

The Greeks got their mythology from the Egyptians, as scholars attest, and through the Greeks the Indians derived their mythology. Pictures of Krishna show him holding a great serpent in his hands and crushing its head with his heel. Again, it is nothing but a repetition of the story of Nimrod, the virgin-born seed of a woman. We now can see that this has passed into virtually every mythology of the nations of the world. So, rather than the myth being the source of the biblical concept of the virgin birth of Christ, it is the biblical concept of the virgin birth (preannounced in the *Protoevangelium*) that is the source of all of the pagan mythological views. Instead of refuting the concept of the virgin birth, these myths establish its validity. All of the various objections to the virgin birth fall by the wayside.

We might add one more objection, and that is Mary herself.

Mary could have stopped the crucifixion, for Jesus was crucified simply for one reason: He claimed that God was His Father. But if it were a lie, and Jesus were not virgin-born, then she could have stepped forward at any time and said, "I will tell you who His father is!" She could have destroyed His whole mission and saved Him from the cross.

There is not a caring mother anywhere who, to save her own reputation, would allow her son to be horribly mutilated and killed. No! But the reason Mary did not raise any objection is that Jesus is the virgin-born, divine Son of God, the Redeemer of men.

May our prayer be, "O Holy Spirit, thou generator of Christ, regenerate me." Wonder of wonders, by the power of that same Spirit, Christ may be born in our hearts today. This God-man came into the world to die in our stead upon the cross, to vicariously pay for all of our sins, to endure in His own body and soul the wrath of His Father for us, to take away our guilt and punishment, to procure for us eternal paradise. May this Christ come and be born in our hearts. May He who was born in a stable come into the sinful hearts of men and be born in us. That is the great wonder. It is still true that:

> Though Christ a thousand times
>   in Bethlehem be born,
> if He's not born in thee
>   thy soul is still forlorn.

Has the virgin-born One been born in you?

CHAPTER 5

Suffered Under Pontius Pilate

*"Then [Pilate] released . . . Barabbas unto them:
and when he had scourged Jesus, he delivered him to
be crucified."*

Matthew 27:26

WE NOW COME to the very heart of the Creed—to the very
heart of Christianity—to the Holy of Holies in the ministry of
Jesus Christ. It is all summed up in one single, somber, solitary
word, a word that stands out in all of its solemnity and dignity,
one comprehensive and emphatic word: He *suffered*. He suffered under Pontius Pilate. He was a man of sorrows and acquainted with grief—a man who suffered and died.

It is amazing to note that the Creed makes a tremendous
leap from the birth of Christ to His suffering and death, passing over His entire ministry. There is not a word in all of the
Creed about His great teachings, about His marvelous example, about the incredible miracles which He performed. All of
this is passed over in silence and immediately we are ushered
into the realm of His suffering and death.

However, this might not be so strange when we consider the
New Testament itself. There we find, if we look at the epistles
of Paul, that virtually the entire ministry of Jesus Christ is ignored. There is no mention of His ethical teachings, and no
mention of a Sermon on the Mount, which liberal theology has
exalted into a virtual substitute for the gospel of Christ. And
no mention of His miracles or His parables. The emphasis is always upon His suffering and death and resurrection. It is even

so in the Gospels themselves, which are the only New Testament writings about His life. One third of each of the first three Gospels deals with His sufferings and death and fully half of the Gospel of John has to do with the last week that Christ lived.

Born, suffered, and died! The position of this phrase in the Creed is worthy of our notice. We have just read that He was conceived by the Holy Spirit and born of the virgin Mary; a *holy* Spirit, a *virgin* Mary, a pure, innocent, and spotless life!

Plato and the rest of the Greeks worshiped truth, goodness, and beauty. Long before Christ came, they said man's sin derived merely from his ignorance. They declared that if only they could see a perfect example of ethics, morality, purity, and piety, they would, no doubt, fall down and adore it and follow it breathlessly. But when He came—the very incarnation of goodness and purity, with a sinless and spotless life, the perfect Christ, the Crystal Christ, the peerless One—man in all of his depravity took Him and nailed Him to a cross. And buried Him out of sight!

No clearer commentary on the nature of the human heart can be found anywhere in the world than in the fact that the pure, virgin-born, spirit-conceived Christ, the peerless One, was hated and despised and crucified. Truly, man is seen with all of his blemishes, wrinkles, warts, and twistedness when we compare Him to the purity of Christ.

We are told that we are to love Him, to trust Him, to follow Him, to obey Him. Yet how hopeless it all seems—to try to be like Him and yet to know that we are so unlike Him. To be like Him, we must have His power. But His power comes only through His death. That is why the emphasis of the Gospels and the Epistles, and the emphasis of the Creed is upon the death of Jesus Christ—and why the central symbol of the Christian Church is His Cross. He *suffered* under Pontius Pilate.

The world in which we live is a suffering body, and it needed a suffering head that could empathize with its pain and agonies. So He came, the suffering Savior to His passion. We read that he was exceeding sorrowful unto death. We read of His loneliness, His agonizing prayers, His disappointment with His disciples, His bloody sweat, the traitor's kiss, the binding with cords, the blows to the face, the plucking of His beard, the spitting, the buffeting, the mocking, the scourging, the crown of thorns, the heavy cross, the Via Dolorosa, the exhaustion, the collapse, the stripping, the nakedness, the impaling, the jeers of His foes and the flight of His friends, the thirst, the darkness, the rejection, and forsakenness by His Father. And finally, the blackness of death. Indeed, He was a man acquainted with grief. *He suffered.*

The Reason for Emphasis

But why the emphasis on these things? Only recently I again read that remarkable speech given at the funeral of Caesar by Mark Antony in Shakespeare's *Julius Caesar.* Antony had secured the permission of Brutus, that "honorable man" so to speak, to tell the people that he "came not to praise Caesar but to bury him," or at least so he said. But in truth he had very different intentions. He told of the goodness of Caesar, his benevolence toward the people, and his desire for their welfare. Finally he held up the rent and blood-splattered tunic of Caesar and, pointing to the various wounds, described how here the dagger of Cassius pierced his body through, and there came the blade of the envious Casca, and here, almost to the heart, plunged the dagger of Brutus and out flowed Caesar's blood as if pursuing the blade. Why did he do that? He did it because he wanted to excite the mob to vengeance for these cruel deeds.

So, too, the sufferings of Christ that are held up before our eyes would excite us to vengeance. Against whom? Against the simony of Caiaphas, the perfidy of Judas, the cowardice of Pilate? No! They had their part, of course. But behind their hands *our* arms may be seen. It was for *our* sins that He died to incite within our breasts a spirit of revenge against our own sins—our sins which placed Him there upon the cross so that we might see sin as it really is in all of its heinousness. And seeing it, hate it, and hating it, despise it and turn from it in repentance.

He suffered. "He suffered under Pontius Pilate," we are told; and in that one statement the Creed is taken out of the misty air and nailed down into the cold rock of history. "Under Pontius Pilate." We have, therefore, no finely conceived fable or cunningly devised myth, but rather we have hard, cold history.

Josephus, the Jewish historian of the first century, said: "And when Pilate, at the instigation of the principal men among us, had condemned him to the cross. . . ." Tacitus, the principal historian of the Romans of the first century, said, as attested: "Christ was put to death as a malefactor by Pontius Pilate in the reign of Tiberius." Pontius Pilate is every bit as much an historical character as is Tiberius Caesar, and we can no more doubt the former than we can doubt the latter. Indeed, on several occasions in the Holy Land I have observed and touched with my own hands the "Pilatus" Stone which was the cornerstone of the great stone yard created by Pilate. This is no myth, no fable, but hard history bound down in time. "He suffered under Pontius Pilate" and "was crucified," we are told.

Born to Die

The Old Testament gave various adumbrations and intimations that this is the way that it would be: Isaac carried the wood upon which he was to be laid in sacrifice up Mount Moriah; the brazen serpent was lifted up in the wilderness where sin itself was held up for people to look to and be healed; the paschal lamb was to be slain and not a bone of its body was to be broken. (If Jesus had been killed by the Jewish method of stoning, many of His bones would have been broken. But He, as that paschal Lamb of God, was to suffer not a bone to be broken.)

The Old Testament makes it even clearer in the words of David when he lamented the fact that they "pierced my hands and my feet" (Psalms 22:16), prophetically describing the death of Christ. And in Galatians, Paul utters that awful execration against all of those who are crucified, saying, "Cursed is everyone that hangeth upon a tree," drawing upon an Old Testament statement (Galatians 3:13, Deuteronomy 21:23).

Crucifixion—the most awfully excruciating, the most painful, the most shameful and ignominious of deaths! But Jesus was crucified. To what end? That He might be dead. Suffered, crucified, dead. The Creed essentially tells us that He was born and that He died. Christ's death is emphasized because the death of Christ was the greatest act and event of His entire life. He is the only person ever to have lived upon this planet who was born for the specific purpose of dying. *He was born to die.* He was crucified in the mind of God before the creation of the world, we are told. That is why He came. Death did not end the work of Christ. Death *was* the work of Christ. We refer to the finished work of Christ when He finished His passion in Death.

Proof that Jesus Did Die

The creedal statement that He died reminds us of the reality of His death. This was no swoon. He did not merely faint, as Mary Baker Eddy and Hugh Schonfield and others have said. He was dead, as was attested by the centurion who dealt in death and had placed many people in its jaws. And if there were to be any doubt, the centurion took his Roman spear and plunged it into His side, piercing the heart, out of which flowed, John tells us, blood and water—undeniable evidence of His death. Many centuries before the circulation of the blood had been discovered, John gives us proof positive that Christ had died, making it plain that not only had death occurred, but also that the circulation of the blood had ceased. It had already divided into its constituent parts of the red blood cells and the watery serum. Out came blood and water. He was dead!

The idea that He merely swooned is, on the surface, obviously an absurdity. Consider: could He have been scourged, a punishment which in itself often produced death . . . could He then be pierced in His hands and feet and left upon a

cross for six hours . . . His side opened by a large Roman spear
. . . be laid in a tomb and wrapped in graveclothes, and then
rise from the dead inside of that tomb, and with pierced hands
roll back a stone weighing many tons, and then walk on
pierced feet all the way to Galilee and climb a mountain and
show Himself as the risen Lord of glory?

Jesus Christ was dead! Dead and buried, says the Creed. So
it was that He was conceived in a virgin womb, and buried in a
virgin tomb, where never a man had lain before. He experienced it all for us.

Every one of us will see the day when we shall be placed in a
coffin and the lid be closed over our face. They will then lock
that coffin and take it to a cemetery, where it will be lowered
into a dark, dank grave. And after the last lament has passed
away, they will shovel in the dirt on top of it. Then they will
plant grass and erect a marker. And, after everyone leaves, you
will be there alone in the coldness and silence of the grave. No
one—no one—can help you then but Christ—no other but that
One who could say, "I am he that liveth, and was dead; and,
behold, I am alive for evermore . . ."; ". . . because I live ye shall
live also" (Revelation 1:18; John 14:19). And He shall speak
that great word and the graves will open and the dead will
come forth at His beckoning. He suffered it all for us.

Why Christ Died

We are told in the Creed that He died. We are told when He
died, under Pontius Pilate. And we are told how He died: He
was crucified. But we are not told why He died. And that, perhaps, is most important of all. I never cease to be amazed at
how many millions of people know that Christ died on the
cross yet have no real comprehension of what that really
means. They continue to go their merry way, oblivious of the
true significance of His death. And though they see on the top
of every church and in front of every sanctuary the symbol of
that death, they seem blind to its meaning.

Why did He die? I think that the ingredients of the atonement are three.

The first one is the heinousness of sin. If it were not for the awfulness of sin, then Jesus Christ would never have died. If men were really good, as so many suppose themselves to be, then Jesus Christ need never have died. If we could get to heaven on our own merit, by our own good deeds, then why did Jesus die? If by merely following the Ten Commandments or living by the Golden Rule we could ever enter into paradise, then to what purpose did He suffer on the Cross?

At least in one thing Freud was right when he reached down into the very depths of the id of man and saw in the dark caverns of the human soul all manner of creeping things, all manner of foul thoughts and desires. He concluded exactly what the Scripture had said: that out of the heart of man proceeds all manner of evil, that man is sinful from the top of his head to the bottom of his feet—"total depravity," the theologians call it.

It does not mean that we are as bad as we could be, but it does mean that every part of us is infected with a deadly poison. If you have a cup of pure water and you put into it but a few drops of a fatal poison, the cup does not have to be one hundred percent poison to be deadly. No! There is not one part of it that you can drink without experiencing its pernicious effects. And so it is with sin. It has pervaded our minds and our emotions and our will—no part of our being is not tainted with the foul thing. As a result sin has cut us off from any access to God, and therefore has cut us off from any way into heaven. The bridge indeed is out!

I remember reading of an incident that happened out in the Midwest: A trucker was going down the highway at night, far from the nearest city. Sitting as he was, high in the cab, he soon noticed a car far ahead of him. But suddenly the car's taillights disappeared. And then the same thing happened to the next car. The truck driver was filled with panic and hit the brakes as hard as he could, finally managing to bring the truck to a stop and get it to the side of the road. He got out of the cab, made his way through a drizzling rain to a bridge that crossed high above a river. There he saw that half of the bridge had completely been washed out, the span having collapsed. Quickly he went out onto the road where many cars were coming. Waving his arms, he tried to stop them, but they did not even slow down; he had to leap out of the way to save his own life. One after the other came roaring up onto the bridge and disappeared with a whoosh into the black waters fifty feet below. Swoosh, swoosh, swoosh. There was no other sound. No cry could be heard, just the deep splashing into the water below.

Finally, after fourteen cars had disappeared into the river, he was able to get someone to stop.

So it is with man. He rushes headlong out of this life, oblivious of the fact that the bridge to heaven is out, that "there is a way which seemeth right unto a man, but the end thereof are the ways of death" (Proverbs 14:12). And so he plunges into the pit of darkness and everlasting torment. Going by the thousands, by the millions, silently into perdition. The heinousness of sin makes the Cross a necessity.

The Justice and Holiness of God

Secondly, there are the justice and holiness of God, which are vital to the atonement. The Old Testament makes it very clear: "Holy, holy, holy is the Lord of hosts" (Isaiah 6:3). Holiness is seen as the foundation of His throne. He is of purer eyes than even to look upon iniquity. He will visit our transgressions with the rod and our iniquity with stripes. The wrath of God must inevitably come upon wrongdoing.

The Edinburgh Review, for a number of generations, carried on its masthead these words: "When the guilty is acquitted . . . the judge is condemned." The justice of God demands that the sinner be punished.

Out in the great prairie states a hundred years ago, men often used to make their way by foot across those vast expanses. The one thing they most feared, especially in the late summer and fall when the dry grass stood almost to their hips, was a prairie fire. Sometimes they could see it coming in the vast distance, roaring across the plain, thirty or forty miles an hour, driven by the wind, and there would be no way of escape.

They could not possibly outrun it and there was no place to hide, no tree to climb.

They finally learned what to do: They would simply light a fire right where they were, and then as the wind blew they would back into the burned-out spot. Standing in that blackened spot when the approaching wall of flame hit them, they were safe. The fire would roar around them and go on.

So it is with the wrath of God. The only place of safety is where the fire has already been. And the only place that the fire of God's wrath has already been is at the Cross of Calvary. On that blackened rock outside the city wall, the fire of God's wrath fell upon the Son of God, and Christ endured in His own body and soul all of the penalty for our sins.

God's Love

The heinousness of sin and the justice of God make the Cross an absolute necessity. But neither one of them would have made it a reality without the love of God. The heinousness of sin and the justice of God only make one thing certain—hell for sinful men. But God's love made a Cross. That infinite love of God, that inexhaustible, unquenchable love of God, caused Him to give His own Son, His beloved Son, His dear Son to die in our place.

There have been many theories of the atonement, all of them presenting some element of truth. But I would say that there is one basic doctrine of the atonement, one fact of the atonement that will suffice: the theory of the atonement held by Barabbas. Not a theologian indeed, he was a murderer, a robber, an insurrectionist, and a thief. He was convicted of capital crimes and was sentenced to die. And it was in his place that Jesus died! Barabbas was released at the instigation of the people, but Jesus was affixed to the cross.

I can imagine that when he got out of that prison where he had been languishing beneath Pilate's palace and found out how he had been extricated from a horrible fate, he made his way along that same Via Dolorosa and then on to Golgotha. Once there, he wormed his way through the crowd until he finally stood at the foot of that center cross and looked up at the man on that cross. He might then have said quietly, "Stranger, I don't know who you are, but one thing I do know: You are dying in my place."

If you want to know the meaning of the Cross, I would urge you to go, in your spirit, and stand before that Cross and look up into the face of the God-man and say, "O, Christ, Savior of men, I do not fully comprehend how You are the infinite and finite One, how You the Creator could die for this creature's sin. But one thing I do know: You are dying in my place!"

That is the meaning of the atonement. That is the fact that makes that horrible, fatal Friday good, and brings joy and hope to the world. That is the fact that enables us to lay our heads upon the pillow for the very last time and face eternity with joy and anticipation, knowing that we are coming, not to the tomb, but to our graduation and coronation day. That is the fact which gives all of life meaning and significance, delivering us from our sin and guilt and shame and making us the sons of God, on our way to an inheritance with the saints in light. Ah, that is the greatest fact in all of the world. "He suffered, was crucified, dead and buried." And He did it all for *me* and for *you!*

CHAPTER 6

He Descended into Hell

"Wherefore he saith, 'When he ascended up on high, he led captivity captive, and gave gifts unto men.' (Now that he ascended, what is it but that he also descended first into the lower parts of the earth?)"
Ephesians 4:8, 9

"WE DON'T SAY that in our church. When we recite the Creed we don't say, 'He descended into hell.' In fact," said this sweet young woman, "Our minister never says anything about hell at all."

That's the problem with many churches. It is not so much what they do say. Oftentimes, it is what they leave unsaid. Important subjects like sin and salvation and even hell often are never mentioned at all.

Let's make one thing crystal clear: We didn't put it in; they took it out, because it has been there since the early centuries of the church. The expression can be traced back to the late 300s, to the church of Aquileia; it later became incorporated into what we know as the Apostles' Creed. "He suffered under Pontius Pilate, was crucified, dead, and buried; He descended into hell." The *Descensus ad Infernos* is a part of the Creed and it is a part of the teaching of the Word of God. "Thou wilt not leave my soul in hell," the Scripture says.

A Grim Reality

The subject of hell is not pleasant to talk about. I would much prefer to speak about light and happy things, about life and paradise. Yet, it is there.

69

Something terrible happened at the New London School in Texas a number of years ago. Four hundred students were in the grammar school. Some of them were at recess playing, laughing, running, jumping; some were still in their classes studying the three Rs. The morning was bright and lovely, and only a few fleecy clouds stretched across the azure sky.

Without warning, as if an atomic bomb had gone off underneath it, the entire school blew sky-high and disintegrated into a million pieces, killing all four hundred students and the teachers as well. The grisly scene shocked the entire community beyond measure.

During the subsequent look into the matter one of the ladies said to an investigator, "My husband told me that it was going to happen. Before the explosion he said he knew that it was going to happen because that gas pipeline under the school was of faulty construction. Yes, he told me that it was going to happen."

The man peered deeply into her eyes and said, "You mean to tell me that your husband knew that there was improper construction in the gas pipeline under that school? He knew that and he did nothing about it?" When she reaffirmed what she had said, he told her, "He is a criminal, a murderer to know something like that and to keep it to himself."

A far greater threat looms beneath our feet than a faulty gas pipeline: the lake of fire, a terrible place of weeping and wailing and gnashing of teeth. We should never forget that Jesus Christ, meek and mild, the lover of my soul, the all-compassionate One, He who is love incarnate, talked more about hell than anyone else in the Scripture.

I would be guilty of murder if I failed to proclaim in unmistakable terms that such a reality as hell exists and that there are many rushing precipitously toward it like blind beasts falling off the edge of a cliff. That doesn't mean we have to harp on the subject or be like one preacher of whom it was said that he talked so much about hell, you'd think he was raised there. Nonetheless, the lake of fire is a grim reality.

Where Hell Is

A man came to visit a coal mine one day. He descended with the foreman in an elevator over a thousand feet down the shaft to the depths of the mine. This man talked as they were taken down, and the foreman, who happened to be a Christian, noted the repeated use of profanity and the taking of God's name in vain. As they descended even deeper, the visitor, wiping his brow, said, "Phew, it sure is getting hot. I wonder how far it is to hell?" The foreman replied quietly, "Well, I don't know how far it is; but if this cable snaps, you'll be there in a minute."

"Where is hell?" was the question the skeptic asked a young man who was a recent convert to Christ. The new convert was trying to talk to him about the gospel. "If you know so much about it, tell me where it is." The young man thought for a moment and he said, "Yes, I know where it is, and I'll tell you where it is. It is at the end of a Christless life."

So it is for all those who reject the love and the mercy and the proferred grace of Jesus Christ and His gospel, who live their own way, do their own thing, ignore Christ and His gospel, and finally die impenitently. They find that at the end of their Christless lives there is hell.

The Ordeal of Thomas Welch

Thomas Welch made that discovery to his utter and total astonishment. He was a construction man and just a few years ago he was building a dam thirty miles from Portland, Oregon. He was walking across the trestle fifty-five feet above the water when his foot slipped and he fell headlong for thirty feet until he landed on his head on a beam, bounced off of that, hit another construction beam and then another, and finally fell into the water where his body disappeared.

About ninety people were working on that site, and immediately they stopped their work and began to look for Welch's body at the bottom of the lake. It wasn't until more than forty-five minutes later that they dragged him up from the bottom of the lake. They thought surely that he must be dead. There was no heartbeat. He was not breathing.

However, they began to apply cardiopulmonary resuscitation techniques. Revived, eventually he opened his eyes and said, "What happened?" Welch remembered more clearly than any other hour in his entire life everything which had transpired during that time.

He said he had awakened on the shore of a vast and illimitable lake of turbulent, rolling blue flame. The heat had been almost insufferable. In the darkness around him he had been able to see a number of other people, some he had known, who had died before and now stood there with looks of utter astonishment upon their faces.

Neither he nor anyone else was in the lake yet, he said, but he knew it surely must be his fate. Strange monstrous creatures, half-human and half-something else, appeared and disappeared in the darkness. Abject terror took hold of him, and he spoke aloud without even realizing it, saying, "If I had known that there was such a place as this, I would have done anything to keep from coming here."

There was no escape. The very thought was beyond consideration. Suddenly, he saw a figure of a person clothed in white with a look of perfect serenity and strength in His face. He knew instantly who it must be, but this person was walking in an angle away from him. He thought, "If only I could speak to Jesus perhaps He could help me." Walking away until He was almost out of sight, Jesus suddenly turned and looked right at him. In the next instant, Welch awoke with people working on his body.

Thomas Welch discovered that hell was very, very real, even as Jesus knew and said and experienced.

Three Meanings

Three meanings have been given to the phrase "descended into hell" over the centuries. Though all of them are true, not all three are equally important. Probably the least significant is the idea of a descent into "the unseen world." The word

Hades, one of the words translated "hell," comes from the Greek verb *idein* which means "to see," and is prefixed by the alpha privative, the initial *a,* which negates "to see." Thus we get "the unseen world."

In the case of the body, that sometimes means the grave. In the case of the soul, it means that place which the Old Testament described as Sheol where the souls of the dead departed to. So, one of the meanings is that the body of Christ went into the tomb and that He remained and continued under the power of death for three days. He was truly dead and buried. That is very true, and it is important because the wages of sin is death, and Christ experienced a genuine death for us; but that is not the most important meaning.

Coming more toward the center of the true significance of the phrase is the second meaning: Christ, by His Spirit, went into the unseen world, Sheol, which contained two separate compartments according to the Old Testament—one for believers and another for unbelievers. Jesus went, according to Ephesians 4 and 1 Peter 3, into the compartment of the departed souls of the righteous, those Old Testament saints who had believed in the promised Messiah. He proclaimed to them the victory which He had accomplished upon the cross and the atonement which He had made.

According to Ephesians 4, He that ascended on high is the same one that first of all descended to the lower parts of the earth and took captivity captive and led them on high. He took the Old Testament saints for the first time into the very presence of God in paradise. They had waited long in Sheol for the death of Christ to pay for their sins.

That, too, is a very important meaning of the term, yet it still is not the most significant. To move closer to the bull's-eye we look into the most significant meaning of all—Christ endured the very wrath of God.

Jesus did not suffer the wrath of God after His death, however. He suffered it on the cross. Placing the phrase *He descended into hell* after the term *buried* in the Creed may be explained by the first use of this phrase in the Creed of Aquileia, where the term *buried* is not included and it simply reads "He descended into hell," meaning that He endured the very wrath and judgment of God.

The Day of Wrath

Some would like to put away the concept of divine judgment and retribution for sin, but Jesus was not one of them. Jesus experienced it Himself. Upon the cross, in body and soul, He endured the incredible agonies of crucifixion, which are beyond our explanation or comprehension. But more than that, in His soul He experienced the very infinite wrath of God as the God-man, the *theanthropos*. He in His own body endured the infinite wrath of God for a finite time. He had often spoken of hell and the wrath of God. Upon the cross He experienced it.

It is often said that people, when they die, see their whole lives flash before their eyes in minute detail. Every word, every scene, sharpens into focus. As He hung upon the cross, Jesus saw with the eye of His mind the entire wretched history of a depraved world. In crystal clarity, sin after sin of every human being who had ever lived or would ever live flashed before Him in all of its vileness, its uncleanness, its horribleness. Jesus saw it all, and after His Father extended the cup of wrath before Him, He drank it down, and Christ became sin for us.

That was the hour and power of darkness.

Some have said that when it became dark at noon, it was an eclipse; they are either ignorant or have forgotten that Christ was crucified at Passover, Eastertime, the time of the full moon. It is not possible to have an eclipse of the full moon, for the sun and the moon are on opposite sides of the earth. No eclipse is possible. God said He would cause it to become dark at noon. The prophet Amos reported that God said in that day He would cause the sun to go down at noon and darken the earth in clear day.

Christ stepped into outer darkness and, experiencing that catastrophic curse of Almighty God, He plummeted into the abyss of hell.

It was the great day of atonement. The scapegoat must be loosed into the wilderness. Christ, as the scapegoat for our sins, staggered into the howling wilderness of hell itself. The inexhaustible wrath of divine judgment fell upon Him. He is without the gates of the city; He is beyond the realm of space; He is outside of time, for time has come to a standstill. Christ endured an infinite penalty in a finite time. He descended into hell!

The Earnest of Our Inheritance

Yet we call that Friday "Good." On that day was generated the greatest Good News this world ever heard—that Christ descended into hell so we would be spared, so we would not have to endure the penalty which awaits the impenitent when they come to the end of their lives.

How often people say, "Oh, I believe we have our hell right here on earth." My friends, only at Calvary was hell ever here on earth. Hell was in session on that center cross on that blackened hill of skulls outside the city wall.

Hell right here on earth? There is an element of truth in that. The Bible says we have the earnest of our inheritance—the earnest of our inheritance! We know what "earnest money" is. When you put down earnest money on a house you are going to buy, it is a promise that there is more to come! We have the earnest of our inheritance now.

The Greek word is *arrhabon* and it comes originally from a piece of cloth. When a person would go to a Greek tailor and buy a piece of cloth to make draperies for the home or covers for a chair or whatever, there would be a great roll of material, and she would cut off a little swatch. The woman would take it home and hold it up to the walls and to the other furniture to see if it matched and fitted the decor. That piece of cloth was the "earnest."

We do receive a bit of that *arrhabon* right here. You who have declared that you have your hell right here on earth, listen carefully to what God is telling you. He is telling you that the whole roll waits for you when you die. You can deny it;

you can ignore it; you can rail against it; you can mock it, but you might as well rail against the Atlantic Ocean for all the good it will do. It is there! The only hope we have is that Jesus Christ experienced it for us. Come to the cross. Lift up your eyes and look upon Him who, on Calvary's hill, descended into hell.

There is the central glory of the Christian faith. May the flag of Christ, with its emblazoned cross, ever wave over land and sea. May there be inscribed upon it in characters of light: He Descended into Hell That We May Never Know Its Terrors and That We May Ascend to Paradise Through Him.

CHAPTER 7

He Rose Again from the Dead

"For I delivered unto you first of all that which I also received, how that Christ died for our sins according to the scriptures; and that he was buried, and that he rose again the third day according to the scriptures."

1 Corinthians 15:3, 4

TEN YEARS after the cessation of World War II, a most remarkable phenomenon continued in Brazil. Quite a few emigrés from Japan were living in Brazil, and on one matter they could be divided into two distinct and hostile camps. On the one hand there were those who accepted the fact that the war was over, that Japan had lost and had surrendered. But on the other hand, another group of Japanese refused to believe such a story. The first group based its conclusions on newspaper and radio reports and on interviews with Japanese relatives and friends who had gone to Brazil from Japan since the war. The other group based its conclusions on the presupposition that the emperor of Japan was divine and, consequently, the Japanese military forces were invincible. The idea that they could either lose or surrender was utterly inconceivable and unacceptable. Their presuppositions would just not let them believe that the war was over.

You may say, "That is mighty strange. How could anyone be so ignorant as to refuse to accept such obvious facts?"

We live in a time when many people take exactly the same position as that latter group of Japanese. They do so with respect to the resurrection of Christ. They base their conclusion merely upon their presupposition.

For example, Rudolph Bultmann, the radical New Testament critic, made this statement: "An historical fact which involves a resurrection from the dead is inconceivable." According to his presuppositions, it could not possibly have happened. No amount of evidence was going to change his mind. It was already well made up. He took the attitude of those who say, "Don't confuse me with the facts. My mind is made up."

Unfortunately, many skeptics of this sort do not realize the blinding effects of their presuppositions, and they operate as if they had no presuppositions at all. One writer has said that naturalism is in our bones—that we have a great deal of difficulty accepting anything which is supernatural because of this infection of naturalism.

Paul faced the same thing when he tried to get King Agrippa to change his presuppositions, to examine the prejudices which blinded his eyes. Paul said to him, "Why should it be thought a thing incredible with you, that God should raise the dead?" (Acts 26:8). Indeed, if we are willing to forget our presuppositions and examine the evidence objectively, the resurrection of Christ becomes something which is obviously true. It has been examined by some of the best authorities in the world—authorities most qualified to make such an examination and to do it painstakingly.

Lord Lyndhurst of England at various times was the Solicitor-general of the British government, the Attorney General of Great Britain, the High Chancellor of England, and the High Steward of the University of Cambridge. This one person in one lifetime held the highest offices ever conferred upon any judge in the history of Great Britain. When he died there was found among his papers this statement: "I know pretty well what evidence is . . . [that has got to be the understatement of the century—indeed a mark of great humility for a man who held those positions] and I tell you such evidence as that for the resurrection has *never* broken down yet."

Or again in Great Britain, Lord Darling, the Chief Justice of England, said, "No intelligent jury in the world could fail to bring in a verdict that the resurrection story is true."

On this side of the Atlantic, Professor Simon Greenleaf, the Royale Professor of Law at Harvard, has considered the evidence for the resurrection. He is considered the greatest authority on legal evidences in the history of the world; his monumental three-volume treatise on the laws of evidence has been the finest statement on that subject ever written. Dr. Greenleaf would be considered a hostile witness; he was a nonbeliever in the resurrection. He was, in fact, a Jew. He applied all of the critical acid tests to every thread of evidence for the resurrection of Christ. And when he concluded this laborious task, he wrote this statement: "If the evidence for the resurrection of Christ were set forth before any unbiased jury in the world, it would be concluded that the resurrection was absolutely an historical fact."

Those are the opinions of three of the most qualified men in history. Christ's resurrection deserves our examination because it is either the cruelest deception and illusion ever to plague the minds of men, or it is the greatest single fact in the history of mankind. All of our hopes depend upon it. You may examine the religions and philosophies of the world and you will find no more than mere speculations and wishes. Only in Christ, against the cold rocks of that empty tomb, can our doubts and fears of the grave be dashed into pieces.

The resurrection of Christ, even as one of the great critics of the gospel said, is the center of the center of Christianity. It is the pillar upon which all else stands or falls. Every unbeliever, from Celsus to Wells, has aimed his mightiest blows at the resurrection. Yet, still it stands like a great rock in the midst of a pounding sea—all of the waves of unbelief and criticism through two thousand years have beat against it. But like a mighty Gibraltar, it stands unfazed and untouched by all of the criticism. Jesus Christ rose again from the dead!

All of our hopes rest upon that fact. Without that there is nothing but dreariness and hopelessness to which we may look forward. Our loved ones are gone, to be seen no more. Children who have died will never be held again. There is no hope beyond the mortician's bench. The darkness, the silence of the tomb is the final abode of all.

Spiritual or Bodily Resurrection?

As unbelievers outside the church have aimed their largest guns here, so within the church the liberal clergy, those apostles of modernity, those unbelievers in clerical garb, have done their best to destroy the resurrection of Christ. They have reduced it to a spiritual resurrection. And they will wax eloquent on the glories of the supposed "spiritual" resurrection of Christ. I am sure that some of you have sat in some churches and heard sermons which have talked about the fact that Jesus' spirit rose and continues on in the world—and, of course, His body remained in the grave.

Well, I wonder what Plato would have thought about that. And I wonder how many people who are thus deceived realize that all of the pagan religions of antiquity taught an immortality of the soul. The distinctness and uniqueness of Christianity is that it teaches the resurrection of the body—that there is concrete, tangible, visible evidence that life goes on beyond the dead. I wonder if Plato, who believed in the immortality of the soul, also believed that the soul would one day flee like a fleeting bird out of the cage of the flesh and take off into the heavens above? The Greeks looked forward to that great emancipation from the flesh. Of course, the idea that the body would rise was repugnant to any Greek, especially to the Platonists. I wonder what Plato would think if he were to sit in one of these sophisticated modern churches and hear the preacher expatiating on the spiritual resurrection of Christ. It seems to me that perhaps four questions might come to his mind:

"First, *why all of this fuss about Christ and His spiritual resurrection?* Why such an ado about Him? Is not, indeed, a spiritual resurrection, as you call it, that which happens to every last person who dies? So why is Jesus any different from anyone else? Why talk about Him?

"Second, *why do you call it a resurrection?* His spirit never died at all. It simply continued to live, free from the shackles of His body.

"Third, *why do you celebrate it on Sunday?* Isn't it true that His spirit was set free on Friday? And is not Sunday the day that those who believe in the resurrection of the body celebrate?

"And, fourth, *why do you call yourselves Christians? In fact, are you not really Platonists and followers of mine?*" And so they are!

No, Jesus went to great lengths and great pains to convince His disciples that He was not a spirit. "Handle me, and see," He said, ". . . a spirit hath not flesh and bones, as ye see me to have" (Luke 24:39). Jesus rose bodily from the dead! And that is the great hope that the Christian faith has.

The Evidence

What is some of the evidence that attests to this fact? As I studied some twelve or fifteen books in preparation for this subject, I was struck again with the immense volume of evidence that is available. After all of that studying, I stood dazed in front of such a mass of material and I thought, *How in the world will I ever be able to convey it to you?* Indeed, it would require several volumes to begin to deal adequately with the evidence. But here I would just like to skip a stone across the ocean of evidence and touch upon a few of the evidences for it.

The Christian Church

As it has been well said, "The Grand Canyon was not created by an Indian dragging a stick." And the Christian church, the largest institution that has ever existed upon the earth, with over 1,350,000,000 professed adherents, was not created by a myth or legend. Indeed, I might claim that Karl Marx never lived or wrote, and yet someone hearing that would point to the massive institution of communism and say, "Then from whence came this?"

So it is with Christ. The Christian church began with the

preaching of the resurrection of Jesus Christ. Every secular and unbelieving historian will grant that is true. Read, for example, H. G. Wells, the famous skeptic and critic. In his *Outlines of History* he deals with the life, ministry, and death of Christ in one chapter and then begins a new chapter with the fact that the Apostles began to preach that Jesus Christ rose from the dead. He says that it was on the basis of that preaching that the church came into existence. And right he is! In fact, all of the sermons, virtually the entire New Testament, reach their culmination point in the resurrection of Christ. All five of the sermons in the Book of Acts by the Apostle Peter—preached to the enemies of Christ and to unbelievers—center in the resurrection of Jesus Christ.

How is it that these Apostles, who just a few days before were craven cowards, cringing within the upper room behind locked doors, now stand boldly and preach to the Sanhedrin? What changed them? Since Wells's presuppositions do not allow him to believe in the resurrection, he must find some other explanation. What is it? Here again, I am constantly amazed at the incredible lengths to which unbelievers will go to try to explain away the resurrection. Their theories are so ludicrous. Wells says: "It began to be whispered abroad that Jesus rose from the dead. First it was whispered by one . . . then it was picked up and whispered by another . . . and someone else said, 'Have you heard He rose again from the dead?' . . . and so it was taken by another . . . then the Apostles began to say the same thing as they preached and so . . . the Christian church came into existence." Isn't that wonderful? How stupid does anybody have to be to believe that?

As every historian knows, the church was born right there in Jerusalem, soon after Jesus Christ was crucified. Did it ever occur to anyone to simply walk a few hundred yards outside the city wall and examine the tomb, to see if this rumor were true? No! Indeed, these people gave their whole lives over to a rumor. They even endured painful deaths because of that rumor. The idea is really too ludicrous to be examined more fully. The church of Jesus Christ is a great testimony to the fact that Jesus Christ rose from the dead.

Testimony of Eyewitnesses

Jesus appeared on ten different occasions, over a period of six weeks, to a vast number of witnesses: to a woman here, to several women there, to two men on the way to Emmaus, to ten Apostles in the upper room, to eleven when Thomas appeared the following week, and to a number of them by the Sea of Galilee where He fixed breakfast. He appeared in the morning and in the afternoon and in the evening. He appeared indoors and outdoors. He appeared over and over again to them. He appeared to over five hundred people at one time. And the testimony of these eyewitnesses is overwhelming!

When you stop to think that if each of these witnesses was brought into a courtroom and assumed the witness stand, and if they testified for only thirty minutes about what they had seen and heard and experienced—then you would have over two hundred fifty hours of testimony. Add to that the testimony of the others who saw and heard Him after the resurrection—then you would really have an overwhelming case. Can you imagine any courtroom, where over five hundred witnesses were brought in and testified to the very same thing (that they had seen it and heard it and experienced it themselves), what the attitude of the jury would be? Well, this is what happened with Christ.

If that is not convincing enough, may I remind you that the Apostles sealed their testimony with their own blood. They suffered torture, the most grievous to flesh and sinew, and they sealed their statements with their very lives. It is an historic fact—and a psychological maxim—that no one willingly gives his life for what he knows to be a fraud. Of course, many people have died because of fraud; many people have died for things which were not true. But it has never been known that any person gave his life for what he *knew* not to be true.

Surely, when Peter hung, crucified upside down upon a

cross, it might have occurred to him (as it might have occurred to all of the others as they endured these cruel and hideous deaths) that the time had come to call it quits and say, "Wait a minute, fellows, I was just kidding. It really didn't happen that way at all."

The idea that they themselves were deluded and deceived has been raised. But this was not a conjuror's trick done on a stage in the far distance and in the dark, because, over and over again, He appeared unto them. He ate with them. "Handle me," He said. He showed them His hands and His side. To Thomas, He said, "Reach . . . thy finger, and behold my hands; and reach hither thy hand, and thrust it into my side: and be not faithless, but believing" (Luke 24:39; John 20:27). "What we have seen with our eyes and heard with our ears and handled with our hands, we declare unto you," they said (*see* 1 John 1:1, 3).

The resurrection, by its very nature, is not something about which someone could be mistaken. You might be easily deceived by a magician, by a conjuror, or by some esoteric philosophy; but could I convince you that your husband does not exist or that your children never were? Of course not! All of the arguments, sophisticated as they may be, would never put a dent in your conviction that that is so. You have seen and heard and handled and you know of what you speak!

The Empty Tomb

Marx and Lenin have their tombs as shrines, as do Muhammad and Napoleon and so many others. The tomb of Christ is empty! And on that empty tomb many a false theory of the resurrection has stumbled and fallen.

The ideas that the Apostles merely had hallucinations, that there was mass hypnotism, or that there was a spiritual resurrection—all of these flounder before the empty tomb. What happened to the body? Where is the corpse? Someone has said that either the Jews or the Romans stole it away. If that were true, when the Apostles began to preach just a few days thereafter that Christ had risen from the dead, why did the Jews go to such lengths to have them arrested, to beat them, to imprison them, and to threaten them with death—and finally to begin killing them? And why did the Jews exhort them to stop preaching in the name of Christ and to stop declaring that He was the Lord of Glory? All of the Jews' threats and punishments and tortures were in vain. The Christians continued to proclaim the gospel. Three thousand were converted, then five thousand, and then a vast multitude—they grew exceedingly.

But, of course, since the Jews or the Romans had the body stashed away in the back room or buried among the roses, it never occurred to any of the cunning members of the Sanhedrin or the high priests to simply haul it out and hang it up by the heels in the town square and say, "There is your glorious Messiah. Take a whiff." It would have been a stink through the heart of Christianity and you never would have heard of Christ. But they could not because they knew not where the body was.

Others say: "The disciples took the body away." Did they? That's what some say. That was the very first explanation that was given of the resurrection. You remember the high priest gave much money to the Roman guards when they came in and suggested, "Say ye, His disciples came by night, and stole him away while we slept" (Matthew 28:13).

Now that has got to be the most remarkable thing that I have ever heard in my life. In all of the tens of thousands of court sessions that have been held in the world, no one has been allowed to testify as to what happened while he was asleep! If the soldiers were asleep how could they know that His disciples came and stole the body away? He might have tiptoed out, been carried out by angels, or stolen by who knows who. No, that will not do. Furthermore, the very presence of the Roman custodian or guard forbids any such attitude as that. And that is the next piece of evidence that I would call to your attention: the fact of the Roman guard.

The Roman guard was a fighting unit. It consisted of four to sixteen well-trained and highly disciplined men. Each carried a six-foot spear with an iron point, a three-foot sword at one side, a dagger on the other side of their tunic, and a shield on the left arm. They were highly trained and highly disciplined. It was unlawful for them to sit down on guard duty or to lean against anything. And if they went to sleep on guard duty then, we are told, according to the institutes of Roman military law, that they were to be burned alive with their own clothing. No! A fear of punishment as well as the discipline kept them keenly awake. That such a guard as this would allow someone to come along and steal a body is beyond consideration.

The Christian Sabbath

Consider the Christian sabbath as a testimony to the resurrection. The Jews, you will remember, were strict and zealous sabbatarians. And they celebrated the seventh day of the week. What happened to cause these same Jewish Christians to give up their sabbath and worship on the first day of the week, the Christian sabbath? It was a monumental event: the resurrection of Christ from the dead, the ushering in of a whole new era of the new heavens and the new earth. A new creation!

I don't know of any other event in the history of the world which is celebrated by a memorial fifty-two times every year. This Sunday and next Sunday and the following Sunday and every other Sunday, all over the world, hundreds of millions of people will testify to the fact that Jesus Christ arose from the dead. Even the unbeliever and the atheist, lying in bed at home reading the comics, will testify to the resurrection by the very fact that he doesn't have to work. Why? Because Christ rose from the dead!

The Stone and the Roman Seal

Then there was the great stone that was rolled in front of the door—a stone weighing many tons, which was set in a groove and rolled downward in front of the door. We are told in the New Testament that it was rolled away—but not simply rolled *away*. One word used in some ancient manuscripts is *anakulio,** meaning *to roll up*—back up the hill from which it was

* *anakulio* in ℵ (Codex Sinaiticus) and B (Codex Vaticanus).

rolled down, in front of the door. Another, *apokulio,* means *away from,* at a distance. John uses the verb *airo,* which means to pick up and move away. Some tremendous force moved this enormous stone.

According to the Bezae manuscript at the University of Cambridge, it would have taken twenty men to move such a stone. That stone bears eloquent testimony to the fact that a few disciples didn't overcome an armed Roman guard and move the stone so they could take the body.

And what about the Roman seal? We know from other writings of that period that the Jewish high priest and members of the Sanhedrin, as well as the Roman guard, would carefully inspect the seal when it was placed on a gravestone. And we know from Scripture that Jesus' tomb was sealed. Once the stone was in place it was sealed with sealing wax and stamped with the Roman signet. The Roman soldiers knew that if that seal were to be broken, they would pay for it with their lives, for the penalty for breaking a Roman seal was death.

The Hostile Witnesses

Then there are the hostile witnesses. How often we hear it said that Jesus only appeared to *believers.* The Apostles did not believe in Him when they first heard the women's report; they thought it was only an idle tale. When they saw Jesus they were frightened and thought they saw a spirit.

But there were hostile witnesses as well: His own half-brother, James, who disbelieved His claims of Messiahship most of his life, mocked Him and thought Him to be mad. But we read in First Corinthians that Jesus appeared unto James after the resurrection. James became the head of the church of Jerusalem and gave his life as a martyr for this One whom he had disbelieved most of his lifetime.

And then there is Saul, transformed into the Apostle Paul. Not only was he hostile; he was viciously hostile, a persecutor, delivering Christians to be tortured and killed. He was on his way to Damascus to persecute more. And then he met the risen, glorious Christ and was transformed into the great

Apostle of the gentiles. Hostile witnesses as well are changed by Christ!

Changed Lives

"Lo, I am with you always," He said. And so He is! Here and around the world, today and every day, He is transforming men and women of every nation, tongue, and tribe. He is taking men and women who have sunk into the very depths of sin and transforming them into steadfast and glorious heroes of the Christ—heroes who are willing to give their lives as martyrs for His cause. Because He is alive for evermore!

You can know the ultimate evidence in the laboratory of your own soul when you invite Him into your life. I once asked a complete unbeliever, "You don't believe that Jesus Christ is alive from the dead?" He said, "No, I don't."

Then I said, "I challenge you to invite Him to take over your life, to become the Lord and Master and Savior of your soul."

"But He is dead!" he replied.

I said, "If He's dead then nothing will happen. But if He is alive—ah, if He is alive, then everything will happen!"

I'll never forget as the two of us sat on his couch in his living room, and he began to pray, eyes wide open, saying, "O, Christ, if You are there, if You are alive from the dead, then come into my heart and save me." Suddenly he leaped to his feet and said, "What did you do to me?" I told him, "I didn't do anything to you." He put his hand on the back of his neck and said, "The hair is standing up on the back of my neck. What happened to me? I feel different."

I said, "You just asked the risen Christ to come into your life! Jesus said: 'Where two or three are gathered together in my name, there am I in the midst of them'" . . . 'Behold, I stand at the door [the door of your heart] and knock: if any man hear my voice, and open the door, I will come in . . .'" (Matthew 18:20; Revelation 3:20).

My friend, He will come into you if you will invite Him to be the Savior of your life, to forgive you your sins: if you repent of those sins, He will take His proper place on the throne of your heart. He will come in and make all things new. He will wash you whiter than snow. He will take away the burden of guilt, and He will take away the despair of the grave. He will give you a never-dying hope and the certainty that when you give up your life in this world you will simply enter into a more glorious life in paradise. Yes, my friend, Jesus Christ rose again from the dead—and He is alive for evermore!

Let all of the doubters and the skeptics and the unbelievers mourn their doleful creed:

> Now He is dead! Far hence he lies
>   in the lorn Syrian town,
> And on His grave, with shining eyes,
>   the Syrian stars look down.

But the Christian sings a far different song, a song which vibrates with hope and joy and certainty:

> Up from the grave He arose,
>   with a mighty triumph o'er His foes;
> He arose a Victor from the dark domain,
>   And He lives forever with His saints to reign.
> He arose! He arose!
> Hallelujah! Christ arose!

CHAPTER 8

He Ascended into Heaven

"And when he had spoken these things, while they beheld, he was taken up; and a cloud received him out of their sight."

Acts 1:9

"HE ASCENDED into heaven"—so states the Apostles' Creed. But most of us have never heard a sermon on the ascension. I am afraid that it is a part of the gospel message that is usually overlooked or downplayed. I think that frequently it is considered something of an epilogue on the gospel of Christ, an addendum to the scheme of salvation, an afterthought by the God of grace, perhaps a codicil to the last will and testament of Christ.

The Ascension Story

This event, however, is one of the basic pillars on which our salvation rests. These pillars are four in number. They are the incarnation, the crucifixion, the resurrection, and the ascension of Christ. Let us look at what is meant by that phrase: "He ascended into heaven."

It was now forty days after Christ had risen so magnificently from the tomb. During those forty days, on ten different occasions Christ had appeared to the disciples, but He lived an otherwise mysterious and aloof life, unseen by human eyes. But now that the forty days were up He gathered the disciples together for the last time at some undesignated spot in Jerusalem and held intimate communion with them. Then He led them forth, as He had so many times during His ministry, out of the city of Jerusalem, across the Kidron valley where He had been brought, bound by the temple police, not too many weeks before. Up the Mount of Olives He went—up a path that I myself have trod, as have some of you—to the top of the Mount of Olives. Then He went a little farther, to the small village of Bethany, and there, as He gathered His disciples once more around Him in a circle and gave them His final instructions, He uttered the great commission: "Ye shall receive power, after that the Holy Ghost is come upon you: and ye shall be witnesses unto me both in Jerusalem and in all Judea, and in Samaria, and unto the uttermost part of the earth" (Acts 1:8).

Luke tells that He then lifted His hands and began to bless them, and as He blessed them, while they looked on, before their astonished eyes, He suddenly began to rise up out of their midst. As they followed Him with their eyes, soon He was above their heads and His words continued to fall like the very dew of heaven upon their heads. When He was a great distance above them, at last a cloud, like the chariots of heaven, received Him out of their sight—as if the great veil had fallen behind the high priest as he entered into the Holy of Holies. And Jesus was gone!

The Apostles were overwhelmed and astonished by what had happened: they had seen Him, flesh and bone, rise up before their eyes and disappear into the sky. They stood gazing into the clouds where He had disappeared.

Then behind them there came a voice, and turning they saw two men dressed in white, angelic messengers sent by God. (It was an angel that brought the proclamation that He was to come to Mary; angels gave the good news to the shepherds there in Bethlehem; angels ministered to Christ in His temptation; angels again succored Him there in Gethsemane; angels made the proclamation and rolled back the stone at His resurrection.)

And now at His ascension, once again it is angels that speak: "Ye men of Galilee, why stand ye gazing up into heaven? This same Jesus, which was taken up from you into heaven, shall so come in like manner as ye have seen him go into heaven" (Acts

1:11). And with that the disciples returned to Jerusalem rejoicing in their hearts. This was the beginning of an entirely new phase: Jesus Christ had finished His work and had gone back to the Father even as He had said He would.

The Significance of the Ascension

That's the story of the ascension. What does it mean? What is the significance of it?

First of all, let's consider what it means to Christ Himself. It meant a great deal to Him. It meant that His mission was accomplished. It meant the culmination of His redemptive work, the completion of His incarnation, the end and reward of His sufferings, and His entrance upon a new and greater sphere of work. It was the beginning of His great intercessory work in heaven above.

For Christ, it was the realization that now at last it was all over and His earthly sojourn was past. He ascended from the earth, through the heavens (the Scripture says "through the heavens of the heavens" until he was far above all things, above dominions and thrones and principalities and powers, until He was at the very right hand of God Himself, "far above all heavens, that he might fill all things." *See* Ephesians 4:10). He had descended but now was the time to ascend.

Theologians divide the work of Christ into two parts. There is, first of all, His humiliation and then there is His exaltation. The humiliation is over. Now the exaltation has come—through the heavens, at last, to be greeted by the angels of God in the heaven above all!

"Lift up your heads, O ye gates," cried the welcoming legions of angels, "and be ye lift up, ye everlasting doors; and the King of glory shall come in" (Psalms 24:7).

And those who watched at the gates of heaven responded, "Who is this King of glory?" And the angelic host answered: "The Lord strong and mighty, the Lord mighty in battle. Lift up your heads, O ye gates; even lift them up, ye everlasting doors; and the King of glory shall come in. Who is this King of glory? The Lord of hosts, he is the King of glory" (vss. 8–10).

Jehovah Himself, the great God of heaven and earth, the second person of the triune God, the Lord of glory, returns from His great conquest below, from His victory over the powers of death and hell and the tomb, from His conquest of sin. He comes back from the howling wastelands of hell itself, entering in to the glory above. His coronation day is at hand! "Lift up your heads, O ye gates; and the King of glory shall come in."

What It Means to Us

We have seen what the ascension means to Jesus Christ. But it means something to us also, because there is a great principle here. Peter tells us that Christ's exaltation after His suffering is the model and pledge and guarantee of His followers' exaltation after persecution and suffering. Down through the ages God has most used those who have suffered most—those who have plunged into the depths are those who have been lifted up to the heights. And there is a great truth here, as it was with Christ who descended a greater distance than anyone had ever descended—from the throne of God to the depths of hell. As the hymnist said:

My Father's house of light,
My glory-circled throne,
I left for earthly night,
For wanderings sad and lone.

Jesus descended farther, out of the throne of glory, down through the ethereal heavens into the darkness of this earth, into the womb of a woman, where He was born to be obedient, obedient even unto death.

As Paul says, ". . . Being found in fashion as a man, he humbled himself and became obedient unto death, even the death of the cross. . . . God also hath highly exalted him, and given him a name which is above every name" (Philippians 2:8, 9). *The secret of exaltation is humiliation.* It is humbling ourselves. "Humble yourselves . . . under the mighty hand of God, that he may exalt you in due time," says 1 Peter 5:6. And so it is down through the centuries that those who have plunged the deepest into humiliation, suffering, pain, persecution, sickness, and sin have been those whom God has lifted up.

Remember Joseph, who was an express type of Christ in the Old Testament? He left his father's home and, betrayed by his brethren, was cast into a pit and sold into slavery. He was delivered to Egypt where he was finally thrown into a dungeon. But from there God lifted him up until He made him sit at the right hand of the pharaoh of Egypt and gave him great and mighty powers.

Or remember David, who plunged into the pit of the sins of adultery and murder—until his bones waxed old within him, until finally God broke him and humbled him and caused him to cry out to God. Then God lifted him up and made him a man after his own heart. Or think of Paul, the persecutor of the church of Christ, who was struck blind and cast down to the ground, but who finally was lifted up to be the great and glorious Apostle to the gentiles.

So it was with Martin Luther, condemned to die at the Diet of Worms, condemned to be burned at the stake, banished, and kidnapped—but finally raised up to be the great reformer of the church.

John Wesley, missionary to America, was a tremendous failure, his words falling on deaf ears and his ministry a flop. He returned to England and almost died on the way; his heart was overwhelmed with the terror of death when the ship almost sank in the north Atlantic. "I came to convert the heathen, but who shall convert me?" he cried. Then, in the humiliation of Aldersgate Street, he heard the gospel and humbled himself; though he was himself a minister and a missionary, he was not yet a Christian. There he received the living Christ into his heart, and God raised him up to be the transformer of England.

So it was with John Knox, from the ignominious ranks of the slaves on a galley ship, he became one who caused the very throne of England to tremble. And so it was with John Calvin, who began his work in Geneva only to have the people turn against him and run him out of the city and out of Switzerland—until finally in desperation they called him back again to do the mighty and world-transforming work that he accomplished there.

Amy Carmichael was cast down onto a bed of pain and long years of suffering and anguish—an invalid, the very last thing she ever hoped to be. And yet, out of that terrible experience there flowed a continuous stream of magnificent poetry. Some of my very favorites and those which have been favorites of others came out of the blackness of that night.

David Livingstone was a complete failure when he entered the ministry. In his first sermon, he came to a point when his memory failed him completely. He stood silently before the people. Long minutes passed by, agonizing and seemingly eternal. Finally, in shame and disgrace he turned and walked out of the pulpit—a total failure. After he recovered himself, he was on his way to the mission field, when the door closed again. But then God opened the door to Africa and lifted him up to a great and magnificent work as the great apostle to Africa who opened the eyes of millions to the gospel of Christ.

Chuck Colson was cast down from a position of might and power, and prestige—into a miserable prison here in these United States. But from there the living Christ raised him up for a tremendous ministry throughout the United States and many other countries today. Joni Eareckson Tada was a thoughtless and flippant young lady until that day when she dived into a lake and found herself lying on her back paralyzed in the hospital. God brought her up out of the despair of that experience and has given her a tremendous ministry. Failure, affliction, persecution, sickness, illness, handicap, pain, heartbreak, disappointment—out of all of that God picks man up and exalts him in His own due time.

The principle is true for Christ and the principle is true for His people: First, there is descent and then there is ascent. First comes the humbling and the humiliation and then comes exaltation. Whatever a person's problem may be, however great seems to be his despair, God can use that very problem to make that person a tremendous asset in the kingdom of God.

Entrance into the Holy of Holies

Christ's ascension means the entrance of the high priest into the Holy of Holies which is above. On the Day of Atonement, once a year, the high priest of Israel, bearing upon his breast and shoulders the names of the twelve tribes, entered into the Holy of Holies. He passed through the holy place and through the veil—that beautifully embroidered veil of blue and purple and scarlet that had been hanging there for so many centuries. The veil was drawn back only once during the year, the only time anyone would dare to enter in beyond the veil. And then only one man, the high priest, could enter; should any other touch that veil, he would be struck dead on the spot.

God was teaching the people of Israel, as He would teach us, that because man has plunged himself into sin, because man has fallen from the grace of God, because man has become filled with iniquity—he can no longer come into the presence of God. As a warning, God has put up a barrier to keep man out, even as the angels with their swords of fire kept out Adam and Eve from the garden. He has warned that you shall not come into His presence. God is of purer eyes than to even look upon iniquity. He is the altogether holy One. His holiness is blazing. Should any sinful, defiled man come into the presence of God, he would be instantly struck dead. "It is a fearful thing to fall into the hands of the living God," the Scripture says (Hebrews 10:31).

Yet, God has not wholly banished His people. He has made a way of access into His presence, but it is a way which is carefully delineated by Him: only by the high priest, and then only once a year, and then not without blood.

When the priest went behind the veil into the Holy of Holies, there stood the ark of the covenant which contained the Ten Commandments engraved by the finger of God and given to Moses on the mount, the rod of Aaron that blossomed, and the pot of manna. Covering the ark of the covenant was the golden mercy seat upon which a golden cherubim stood at either end, their wings outstretched toward one another above the mercy seat. There the high priest sprinkled the blood of the sin offering.

All of this was symbolic of the fact that it is a life for a life, that the wages of sin is death, and that those wages must be paid! Either an innocent substitute will die in our place, or we shall die as we come into the presence of God. So, as the people of Israel waited outside on their knees in prayer, the high priest stood in the awesome presence of the living God who dwelt between the cherubim in a visible Shekinah glory—the very presence of the living God. He went there to provide access for them, that they might pray to Him, that they might have another year, that they might have the benefits of His covenant.

But now, Jesus Christ has gone beyond the veil, the veil of His own flesh, and has entered into the Holy of Holies on high—not that which is made with hands, but into heaven itself, into the throne room of God, where God sits in all of His blazing majesty. He has entered there, not without blood—yes, with His own blood, coming as the sacrifice made for our sins. He is the great priest who has offered Himself for the life of sinners and paid the debt that no one else could pay. He has entered in as the high priest. This is the meaning of His ascension as well.

The Establishment of the Church

We might say that through the ascension of Christ there was brought about the establishment of the church—and the universalization of the church. When Jesus Christ was upon earth He was localized. He was only in one place at a time. And if He had remained on earth, then the church would have remained local, in Jerusalem or Galilee, and not universal as it is now. But He went up on high so that the church might become a universal church. He said, "It is expedient for you that I go away; for if I go not away, the Comforter will not come unto you; but if I depart, I will send Him unto you" (John 16:7).

And so ten days after His ascension, as they waited in that upper room, He poured out the gift of the Holy Spirit upon them. We read that He received and gave gifts to men. He received the gift of the Spirit for us as part of the payment for His ransom and atonement upon the cross. And that Spirit He poured out upon the world for us and created His church.

Intimate Communion

Furthermore, He not only created the church, but He created it to have intimate communion with Him. When Jesus was on earth the multitudes followed Him, but He selected a group of twelve to be with Him. And among them, three—Peter, James, and John—had more intimate communion with Christ. And even within this inner circle, John, the beloved disciple who leaned his head upon Jesus' breast at the last supper, seems to have enjoyed an even closer relationship to our Lord.

But today, because Jesus has ascended on high and because He is present with us by His Spirit in our midst, we have a more intimate and personal communion with Christ than even the beloved disciple John had. We may not merely lean our heads upon His breast; He dwells *within* our breasts, in our very hearts. Christ has come to live and to have intimate daily communion with us. "Behold, I stand at the door [the door of our hearts] and knock: if any man . . . open the door, I will come in to him, and will sup with him . . ." (Revelation 3:20).

You can have that intimate communion day by day at any place, in any land, in any clime, in any language, whoever you may be, whatever your station. You can know Him intimately and personally and sing with the hymnist:

> O Jesus, ever with us stay,
> Make all our moments calm and bright;
> Chase the dark night of sin away,
> Shed o'er the world Thy holy light.

Jesus has gone to prepare a place for us. As our Forerunner, He went to prepare a place, and He took with Him our own human nature, something that He did not bring down from heaven. He came as a Spirit, the *logos,* the second person of the Trinity, but He went back to heaven bearing with Him flesh and bone, our own nature—body, spirit and soul. We know that because our Forerunner was received into heaven, we also may be received there as well. "He ascended into heaven"— this is not just a condition, a state of mind, but, rather, as Jesus said, "I go to prepare a place for you" (John 14:2). The Greek word is *topos,* from which we get *topography,* literally the writing and description of places. And Christ has gone to "a place," we know not where it is, but beyond the farthest stars. There He has prepared mansions of glory for us, to dwell in glorified bodies, with no suffering, sorrow, pain, sickness, or death. One day we shall see Him as He is.

CHAPTER 9

The Enthronement of Christ

"But this man, after he had offered one sacrifice for sins for ever, sat down on the right hand of God; from henceforth expecting till his enemies be made his footstool."

Hebrews 10:12, 13

THE WORDS in the Apostles' Creed—"And sitteth on the right hand of God, the Father Almighty"—express what is known as the "session" of Jesus Christ. This comes from the Latin word *sedere,* which means to sit, even as the session of our church consists of those elders which sit to govern the church. So, Christ sits at the right hand of God, the Father Almighty. As I said in the previous chapter, few sermons are preached on the ascension of Christ. But even fewer have been preached on this subject.

The Meaning

What does it mean that Christ "sitteth on the right hand of God, the Father Almighty"? If you are in a confessional church, you say it every week. But what does that signify? What does it imply? As we take it apart and look at it, I think you will discover that there are tremendous implications involved in this often overlooked phrase. It easily divides itself into three parts: *sitteth, on the right hand,* and *of God, the Father Almighty.*

The fact that He "sitteth" indicates, first of all, a completion of His work of atonement and, secondly, the beginning of His work of intercession.

His work of atonement has been completed! We read in the

New Testament that every priest stands daily, ministering and offering sacrifices which could never take away sins. "But this man, after he had offered one sacrifice for sins forever, sat down on the right hand of God . . ." (Hebrews 10:12).

In the tabernacle created in the wilderness, and again in the temple of Solomon, beautiful furniture was to be found in the holy place and in the Holy of Holies: the table for shewbread, the altar of incense, the great seven-pronged candelabra and, within the Holy of Holies, the ark of the covenant with the glorious golden cherubim. But nowhere, either in the tabernacle or the temple, was there any chair or bench. Why? Because the work was never done. These priests, continually ministering, offered sacrifices day after day for sin. The sacrifices had to be continually repeated, for it was not possible that the blood of bulls and goats could take away sin.

But this man, this Jesus, having offered one sacrifice for sins forever, *sat down* because it was done. It was finished! It was over! So few people seem to understand the simple fact that Christianity is not "do." It is "done." Jesus declared it: It is done! It is paid! It is finished! *Tetelestai!* It is accomplished! The atonement for our sins was paid in full and we can do nothing to add to it.

I recall reading once of a master wood craftsman who had decided to make for his friend a beautiful coffee table. He spent months constructing it, carving all manner of intricate designs around the side of the table, and then finishing the surface with seventeen coats of Parisian finish. It glistened so that you could practically see your face in it. He wrapped it in a soft cloth and brought it to his friend and then carefully removed the cloth. "Voilà!" he said. "There it is! Your long-anticipated gift!"

It was, indeed, a thing of consummate beauty. But his friend said, "Oh, I think it is just magnificent, but I couldn't simply accept it as a gift. You have done all the work. Surely I must do my part." And with that, he picked up a piece of sandpaper and started to sand the top of the table. His friend grasped his wrist and said, "Stop that! You'll ruin it all. *It is finished!*"

And so it is with the great redemption wrought by Christ. It is done! It is finished! It is perfect! *He sat down.* There is nothing that we can add. There is nothing that we can contribute, as if there were anything that we had to contribute. On the one hand, there obviously is nothing that we have to offer, for every day of our life, every page in the book of our life, is stained with sin. And every contribution that we make is really a detraction. On the other hand, nothing is needed, because it is perfect. What can you add to infinity? Christ suffered infinitely upon the cross and paid an infinite price. There is naught that is needed to be added. And if there were, neither you nor I has it to offer.

His atoning work was finished, but He sat down to commence His work of intercession. Christ is our great intercessor with God. And that intercession of Christ's consists, first of all, in His appearing in the presence of God for us and presenting the memorials of His suffering in our behalf.

He is doing the same as the Jewish priests did on the day of atonement when they entered the Holy of Holies behind the veil. They entered not without blood, having first sacrificed for their own sins, and then bringing the blood for the sins of the Jewish people for the year. But if a priest should enter in behind that veil without doing everything precisely as God had commanded, he would have been struck dead instantly. In order for the people to know that the priest was alive within the Holy of Holies, golden bells were sewn into the skirts of the high priest's robe. The tinkling of the bells affirmed that the priest was continuing his ministrations within the Holy of Holies and that he still lived and that the sacrifice for their sins was accepted.

Secondly, the intercession of Christ consists in His answering all of the accusations which are made against us by Satan, who is the accuser of the brethren. Even as he appeared before God accusing Job, likewise he accuses us of all manner of sins. All of our iniquities and all of our transgressions are picked up by this malignant spirit and are hurled before the throne as accusations against us.

Who shall plead our case? Where is the advocate for our defense? Not only does Satan accuse us, but so do all the unbelievers who claim that we do not live up to that ideal which we profess. Those sins are hurled against us also.

Furthermore, at times our own conscience condemns us. Ah, who shall plead our case? Thank God, there is One—at the right hand of God—who is our advocate, who pleads those five bleeding wounds, whose blood ever intercedes on our behalf.

This intercession of Christ consists, thirdly, in His strengthening us against temptation before we have sinned. Remember what Christ said to Peter: "Simon, Simon, behold Satan hath desired to have you, that he may sift you as wheat: But I have prayed for thee, that thy faith fail not..." (Luke 22:31, 32).

As wondrous as it is to be saved, something else strikes me at this point in my life as being even more marvelous. For now the years have rolled by, one after another, until they have mounted up to decades, and those have added up until now almost thirty years have passed since that glorious night when I first met the Savior. There in my apartment He came into my heart and life and delivered me from the burdens of guilt, created a new heart within me, and gave me the free gift of eternal life as I simply rested my soul upon Him and invited Him to live in my life. But the amazing thing to me now is that throughout all of these long and sometimes difficult years, He has been with me, He has never forsaken me, and has kept me in the way everlasting. I am amazed that as weak as I am, I have not been totally overwhelmed by temptation and sin, for I have seen others fall by the wayside. I thank God that He has kept me through these years. How? Well, "I have prayed for thee that thy faith fail not." He is our great intercessor with the Father.

On the Right Hand

He sits *at the right hand.* And what does that mean? Of course, it means the place of honor and favor. It also means not only honor and favor for Himself, but also for us.

First, note for Himself: This One who was once despised and

rejected of men, "a man of sorrows and acquainted with grief" (Isaiah 53:3), now occupies the most exalted position where there is joy for evermore. Jesus Christ, who was derided by sinners, now is celebrated by saints. And the scoffing and the hissing of the reprobate has given way to the panegyrics of angels. He occupies the most honorable position of all. The flailing of whips and the pounding of hammers has been replaced by the flourish of trumpets, the beating of drums, and the flying of colors—as the Son of God has come home to sit at the right hand of His Father. And on his escutcheon are emblazoned in letters of light the words: ". . . power, and riches, and wisdom, and strength, and honor, and glory, and blessing" (Revelation 5:12). "And the four [living creatures] said, Amen. And the four and twenty elders fell down and worshiped him that lives forever and ever" (v. 14). Amen. Jesus Christ is at the place of honor and favor at last.

But not only for Himself—also for us. He is our surety, our representative and our head and headship, which means not only dominion but also union with the body. For we are His body and He is our head. And if He sits at the right hand of God, the Father, so then do we also. The raising and elevation of Christ is not only for Him, but it is also the raising and elevation and acceptance of all believers in Him. The Scripture says: "And [He] hath raised us up together, and made us sit together in heavenly places in Christ Jesus" (Ephesians 2:6). Even now, you and I, positionally in Christ, sit in the heavenly places at the place of honor and favor of God. In Christ, we are seated at the right hand of God, the Father Almighty in the position of honor. That is what it means when we confess that "He sitteth at the right hand of God, the Father Almighty." What great proof this is of our justification, of our noncondemnation! It has been said that the basis of our noncondemnation and justification is that Jesus Christ died for us and that no greater argument could ever be advanced. And what a magnificent argument that is! But there is more, as Paul says in Romans 8:34 not only that He died for us but also, ". . . yea, rather that is risen again." Could any greater argument be advanced than that His resurrection from the dead proves the fact of the acceptance of His sacrifice, and that He indeed rose for our justification? But Paul goes on: ". . . who is even at the right hand of God, who also maketh intercession for us." How glorious is the position of the believer through the exaltation, the ascension, the session, and the intercession of Jesus Christ for us!

Of God, the Father Almighty

Thirdly, we confess that He sits on the right hand of God, the Father Almighty. And this is a guarantee of power and of victory. Jesus said: "All power is given unto me in heaven and in earth" (Matthew 28:18). God stretches forth His hand and none can stay it or say unto Him, "What doest thou?" He works His will among the inhabitants of the earth and the armies of heaven.

All power is given to Jesus Christ. He is the omnipotent One, and His will shall be done on earth as it is in heaven. Though it is coming about so slowly that we often do not now see that it is happening, we do know that it is taking place. His Kingdom is coming upon the earth—the glorious power and victory! We are told that He sat down upon the right hand of God "until I make thine enemies thy footstool" (Hebrews 1:13). Jesus Christ, now and through these last nineteen hundred years, has been continually gaining the victory, a victory which began at the time of His death and resurrection and continues on through the ages.

In A.D. 363, Julian the Apostate, that emperor of Rome who tried to light again the fires of the altars of pagan gods and overthrow the newly-established Christian faith, was on the march against the Persians. In his army, of course, were numbers of Christians. One of these men was being sorely derided and persecuted by some of the heathen soldiers. They mocked him, beat him, threw him to the ground and said, "Now tell me, where is your carpenter now?" He responded: "He is busy constructing a coffin for your emperor." And just a few months later, with a mortal wound in his side, Julian the apostate one took his hands and grasped a handful of his own blood, flung it

against the sky and said, "Thou hast conquered, O Galilean."
Yes, the Carpenter of Galilee is busy constructing coffins for
all the ungodly kings and kingdoms of this earth.

Hitler said that Christianity would be cast out, "root and
branch," and that he would destroy it all. Jesus Christ built his
coffin! So said Mussolini, and Christ constructed another coffin
for him! Even now, our Carpenter will yet make a coffin for
communism. It too shall be swept into the dust heap of history!
And Christ, the conquering hero, shall continue to ride forth
conquering and to conquer. Marx and Lenin, Stalin and
Khrushchev, Andropov and Chernenko, and all of the rest
shall find that Christ, that One whom they so despised, has
been busy making their coffins as well! Not only has Christ
achieved a victory over the forces of evil, but He has also
achieved a glorious victory over death, that last enemy to be
overcome, that chief evil of mankind. Jesus Christ has overcome it.

I saw a grim specter walking up and down, to and fro
throughout the earth continuously reaching out his bony finger
and touching men and women. And when he touched them, in
an instant, the rich became poor, millionaires became paupers,
the well became ill, the young became old, the strong became
palsied. And they all died! And I said, "What is the name of
this specter that walks up and down amidst the earth?" The answer came back: "His name is Death!" For more than forty
centuries this grim tyrant had conducted his ghastly business,
killing men and women and dragging their corpses into his
cold palace. Kings and conquerors had all fallen at his fatal
touch. No one was strong enough to withstand his approach.

Then one good Friday evening there appeared a stranger
outside the doors of that icy palace, a palace filled with bones
(even the chalices on the table were shining skulls). The columns were made of bones, and the beams of the ceiling were of
human bones. Back and forth within that ghastly castle walked
this tyrant who feared no man. And then this stranger stepped
within that cold palace and approached, unafraid, that mighty

tyrant. He grasped him with one hand, lifted him up, threw him to the pavement on his back, and placed upon the tyrant's neck the heel of triumph.

Then this mighty stranger walked amidst the caverns of that castle of death for three days and three nights. Through the labyrinthine corridors of horror he went until he found the two main pillars which held up the whole domain. And he rocked them back and forth until the whole thing began to crumble. Then he took up the ponderous gates, lifting them off their hinges and marched forth with a shout of victory, "I am the resurrection and the *life!*" Our Jesus had conquered death!

And then I saw a beautiful being walking to and fro, up and down, throughout the earth. And this being reached out his hand and touched, first one and then another. And at his touch the poor became rich, the sick became well, the palsied became whole, the blind saw, the deaf heard, and the lame leaped for joy. I said, "Who is that beautiful being that walks through the earth?" The answer came back: "His name is Death, conquered by the King of kings, transformed and conscripted into the very service of Christ on behalf of those whom he loved. He has now been transformed by Christ! Death makes the poor rich; the old, young; the blind to see."

Jesus has conquered death. O that we might praise Him as He ought to be praised, for He sits in magnificent victory at the right hand of the majesty on high. Let the palms be waved, let the crowns glitter, and let our anthems ascend. They cannot tell the half of it! Let the angelic beings—cherubic, seraphic, archangelic—praise Him (but even they cannot describe His glory).

Sing on, sing on, ye hosts of the glorified. And if your songs cannot express it, if your scepters cannot reach it, then let all the myriad of the saved, through all the centuries of time, join in one great, jubilant exultation and exclaim: "Jesus! Jesus! Jesus!" He sits on the right hand of the majesty on High!

I saw a multitude approaching the gates of His city. And as they stood before that great gate made of one single pearl, the voice came forth from within saying, "What is the password?" And a look of puzzlement passed over their faces. They said, "password?" We know no password, but we have been great upon the earth—and we have come to be great in heaven." And a voice rumbled and thundered from the very throne of God! "No!" And the reverberations went down to the golden streets until they caused the very walls of the city to tremble: "I never knew you! Depart from Me."

And others came and, when asked the password, they said: "We know no password, but we have worked hard and done many good deeds. We have fed the poor, visited the sick, and endowed colleges and hospitals. We have come to enter in to our reward." And, again, the streets of heaven reverberated with the sound: "I never knew you! Depart from Me."

There then came others who, when asked the password, responded: "We have been but wanderers upon the earth. We have wandered from God and have been sunk in the depths and the mire of sin. We are unworthy of entrance. We have transgressed the holy law of heaven. We are worthy of death. But then we heard the melodious voice saying, 'Come unto me, all ye that labor and are heavy laden.' And we came to Jesus!" And with that, the bells began to peal, the great gates were flung open, and a voice came saying, "Let those wanderers enter into the city of the King, for the time of their glorification has come."

My friends, the password to paradise is *Jesus,* the One who has paid for it all, the One who intercedes for us daily, the One who has gained the victory, the One who will take us all the way to paradise. For He sits at the right hand of God, the Father Almighty!

CHAPTER 10

He Shall Come Again

"And to you who are troubled rest with us, when the Lord Jesus shall be revealed from heaven with his mighty angels, In flaming fire taking vengeance on them that know not God, and that obey not the gospel of our Lord Jesus Christ."

2 Thessalonians 1:7, 8

"HE SHALL come," says the Creed. This is the unequivocal declaration of the oldest creed of Christendom. It is in the Apostles' Creed, the Nicene Creed, the Constantinopolitan Creed, the Westminster Confession of the Presbyterians, in the Thirty-Nine Articles of the Anglicans, the Augsburg Confession of the Lutherans. It is in all of the great creeds of Christendom. It is found in all of the systematic theologies, the lectionaries, and the hymnals of all of the Christian churches of history. It is part of the great faith of Jesus Christ! *He shall come again!*

The Old Testament distinctly prophesied it. Scores of passages in the New Testament expressly declare it. Jesus Himself told us unmistakably that:

Hereafter shall ye see the Son of man sitting on the right hand of power, and coming in the clouds of heaven.

Matthew 26:64

The Apostles also say we are:

Looking for that blessed hope, and the glorious appearing of the great God and our Savior Jesus Christ.

Titus 2:13

Our conversation [our life] is in heaven; from whence also we look for the Savior, the Lord Jesus Christ.

Philippians 3:20

In that day we are to be:

... unblamable in holiness ... at the coming of our Lord Jesus. ...

1 Thessalonians 3:13

We which are alive and remain shall be caught up ... to meet the Lord in the air: and so shall we ever be with the Lord.

1 Thessalonians 4:17

When the Lord Jesus shall be revealed from heaven. ...

2 Thessalonians 1:7

When the chief Shepherd shall appear ....

1 Peter 5:4

The Apostles declared that there would come scoffers who would deny His coming:

Where is the promise of his coming?

2 Peter 3:4

In reply, Christ averred:

Hereafter, shall ye see the Son of man sitting on the right hand of power, and coming in the clouds of heaven.

Matthew 26:64

In the Apocalypse, the Apostle John declared:

Behold, he cometh with clouds; and every eye shall see him, and they also which pierced him: and all kindreds of the earth shall wail because of him.

Revelation 1:7

Even so, come, Lord Jesus.

Revelation 22:20

This second advent of Christ is the great hope of the Christian. It is to be the final culminating point of history—the great climacteric of the ages. When the last page of the last volume of history shall have been written, there shall be the final exclamation point, and Jesus Christ shall come again. He shall appear in all of His glory in the sky. And in that day the drama of the ages shall be brought to a glorious conclusion.

How will it be? How will He come? Well, let me say that the Apostles' Creed is an effort to unite Christians in those things which are most assuredly believed. Unfortunately, it is true that there have been those who have laboriously worked over their charts and have set their dates for the return of Christ. And others have divided the people of God endlessly on all of the minutiae which are connected to the second coming. But here I would like to fix your attention simply on that great central event which all of the body of Christ has confessed as part of their faith—*He shall come again!*

How He Will Come

Let me say, first of all, how it will *not* be. The Second Advent of Christ is not the coming of Christ into our hearts by faith when we trust in Him for our salvation and receive Him as Lord and Master of our life. No. That is the spiritual coming. The other will be physical. It is not referring to when Christ poured out His Spirit at Pentecost as maintained by some who have tried to evade the clear teaching of Scripture. Nor is it to be considered our going to be with Christ at death, or Christ's coming in great cataclysmic judgments in the history of the world, such as the destruction of Rome. No. All of these are quite diverse and very different from that which is described as the Second Advent of Christ.

Bodily

Just how will He come? I believe that five adverbs describe very clearly that final denouement of history.

He will come, we are told, *bodily*. When Christ led the disciples up the Mount of Olives on that final day of His earthly pilgrimage, after He had proclaimed again the great commission, He lifted His arms in blessing upon them. As they beheld Him, He was taken up until finally a cloud received Him out of their sight. And two angels appeared to them and said, "Ye men of Galilee, why stand ye gazing up into heaven? This same Jesus, who is taken up from you into heaven, shall so come in like manner as ye have seen him go into heaven." How did they see Him go? They saw Him go bodily, physically. And likewise Jesus Christ shall come again.

Visibly

And if He comes bodily, then, secondly, He must obviously come *visibly* so that we may see Him with our eyes, even as Job so many centuries ago declared. The Apostle John, in the last book of Scripture, attests to this: "Behold, he cometh with clouds; and every eye shall see him" (Revelation 1:7). Every eye shall see Him!

Someone has imagined that this is now possible because of television. But that idea is ludicrous. His coming could not possibly be missed. When Jesus Christ comes again in all the glory of His Father, He will eclipse the sun—and every eye shall see Him—not only we who are living but, as Paul tells us, even the dead shall be raised from their tombs. The sea will give up the dead that are in it; that crystal sarcophagus will reveal those who have long lain in the bottom of the sea. The cemeteries will be opened. Westminster Abbey will give forth its honored dead. The catacombs of Rome will disgorge their dead. The mummies of Egypt will be unwrapped and revealed. All of the dead of the ages will be brought forth.

And every eye shall see Him! Judas shall see Him. We are told that those that pierced Him would see Him. And all the kindred of the earth will wail because of Him. Come now, Judas! Now you know where He is. There He is in the midst of the air in all of His glory. Now, run ye, hie ye to the high priests and betray Him once more—for you know where He is. What is the matter, Judas? Will not your legs move? Come now, Caiaphas, tell us once more that it is expedient that this one man die so that the whole nation may not perish. Come! Tell us how we should take Him with rough hands and skewer Him to a cross. Or are your hands so busily engaged in blinding your eyes, blocking the bright effulgence of His glory from your eyes, that you cannot look at Him? Come, now, Pilate. Call for a basin to wash your hands and tell us once more that you will have nothing to do with this man, for no one can find any place where he will have nothing to do with this Man. Indeed, they shall call for the hills to cover them and the mountains to fall upon them to hide them from the face of Him that sits upon the throne, from the wrath of the Lamb. He will come visibly and every eye will see Him.

Gloriously

We can say, thirdly, that He will come *gloriously*. Someone once said to me, "I suppose that if Jesus Christ came again, as some people say He will, and were to walk around Ft. Lauderdale or Chicago or London in a business suit, that we would probably take Him and crucify Him once more." How little he understood what the Second Advent of Christ really means. For Jesus will not come again in humility, in humiliation. He will come this time in glory with the power of His Father, with all of His mighty angels attendant, with ten thousand times ten thousand of His saints, with the sound of a trumpet that shall wake the dead, and with the voice of the archangel.

None will dare lift a hand against Him, for He will come, this time, undisguised. When He came before, He came fully disguised: the disguise seen by the Bethlehem caravansary, the disguise of the mausoleum in stone, the disguise of the seamless robe and the sandals, the disguise of the face, the voice, and the eyes. But this time He will come with His glory unsheathed—and people will see Him as He really is. His glory will eclipse the brightness of the sun. Ten thousand of the most glorious sunsets or sunrises will pale into insignificance when He shall come with a myriad of angels attending.

Look, ye saints! The sight is glorious:
See the Man of Sorrows now;
From the fight returned victorious,
Every knee to Him shall bow.

He will come again, gloriously with clouds, with mighty angels, in flaming fire, with a voice of the archangel, and with the trumpet of God. He will be the most glorious sight that mankind has ever seen.

Triumphantly

Fourthly, He will come *triumphantly,* triumphant over His foes! Those that pierced Him shall wail because of Him. For Christians it will be a day of great rejoicing. But for those who have been unbelievers—when they shall see the glory of His power—then it shall be a day of great wailing. *Dies Irae,* day of wrath, a day of trembling when Jesus Christ shall come again. For the unbelievers, He comes "in flaming fire taking vengeance on them that know not God, and that obey not the gospel of the Lord Jesus Christ: who shall be punished with everlasting destruction . . ." (2 Thessalonians 1:8, 9). Oh, my friends, what if it were today? What if it were today!

Christina Rossetti, the poetess, said that once she was seated in a large audience listening to a magnificent symphony orchestra that was playing magnificent music. And then, all of a sudden, at an instant, every player—with concerted action—reached up and turned the page of his or her music. At that moment she thought, so will it be when the Lord Jesus Christ returns in glory! Every eye shall suddenly—in concert—look up, and every head shall turn to see the coming of the Son of Man. And in that day, how will it be for those that do not believe, for those who have never repented of their sins, for those who have ignored the invitation of His mercy? It will indeed be a day of great fear and anxiety for them when Christ comes triumphing over His foes. They will be destroyed with everlasting destruction!

How will it be for you? We should remember that though the second coming of Christ is certain, it is also uncertain as far as the time is concerned. For we know not the day or the hour. Though some have foolishly tried to set the date, Christ has made it clear that it is kept in His Father's power alone. *We know not.*

Unexpectedly

And so, fifthly we know that His coming will be *unexpected*, in an hour that we think not. Suppose I were to ask you if you thought that Jesus Christ would come today? Have you thought about it since you awakened this morning? You would probably answer no. And yet it should be a source of anticipation and expectation. We should say: "Come, my beloved, come. May this be the glorious day—the day of graduation, of coronation, when we shall see Thee face to face." It could be today!

Since you do not expect Him to come today, then this day becomes a very good candidate. It *could* be now! All of your plans—your carefully laid plans, what you are going to do next week, next month, next year, the next decade, your plans for retirement—may all disappear in an instant should Christ appear today. Unexpectedly, He will come. Like a thief in the night, He will come.

Archibald MacLeish gives us a poem which describes the end of the world in a most interesting way, in a most incongruous way. For he sees the end of the world from the perspective of those who are witnessing a circus.

> Quite unexpectedly as Vasserot
> The armless ambidextrian was lighting
> A match between his great and second toe
> And Ralph the lion was engaged in biting
> The neck of Mme. Sossman while the drum
> Pointed, and Teeny was about to cough
> In waltz-time swinging Jocko by the thumb—
> Quite unexpectedly the top blew off:

And there, there overhead, there, there hung over
Those thousands of white faces, those dazed eyes,
There in the starless dark, the poise, the hover,
There with vast wings across the canceled skies,
There in the sudden blackness, the black pall
Of nothing, nothing, nothing—nothing at all.

What was there? He doesn't say! And I think perhaps that he didn't know, but *we* know, don't we? We know that in that day when the stars shall fall as lead from the sky and the heavens shall be rolled like a scroll, that there in "the canceled sky," in the deepening hole that once was a universe, shall appear the Son of Man in all of His glory.

How will that day be for you? Will it be a day of keen anticipation? Of welcomed delight? Or will it be for you a day of dread and foreboding, a day of unutterable horror, of unspeakable terror, of indescribable alarm? Does it cause your heart to blanch with fear, to start back, to stand aghast, to tremble, and to cower? It all depends on whether or not Jesus has already come, by His Spirit, into your heart: to redeem you, to forgive you, to make you His own, to embrace you in His love, and to forgive you for all of your sins.

Has He come into your heart? *Have* you opened the door of that heart and said, "Come, Lord Jesus, there is room in my heart for Thee"? If so, then that will be the day of days—the day of delight. You will see your Beloved, your long-besought Beloved face to face.

But if you have continued impenitently in your sins, if you have been satisfied with only nominal Christianity, if you have been satisfied to have your name upon the roll and not Christ upon the throne of your heart, if you have rejected Him, if you have spurned the invitation of His gospel—then, for you, it will be the fulfillment of the worst of all your nightmares. For in that day, suddenly, the great day of grace shall close as a huge steel vault door closing forever—closed and ended—*all over for all eternity.* And you will have nothing to look forward to but certain judgment.

But now, at this moment, the day of grace is still open and the word of welcome still goes out. Oh, I would that the overarching heavens could be made into a great crystal bell and all of the myriad of stars could be welded together into one silvery tongue that would swing back and forth until at last it would ring against that crystal bell and its sound would reverberate through all the cosmos until it sets your soul to thrilling with the word: "Come!"

But if you still have not opened your heart on that day, then it will be as though all of the great guns and the great artillery, the sixteen-inch guns and the great cannons all together were to discharge simultaneously with one thunderous, reverberating boom, and the voice would roar throughout your soul: "Go!"

It is a simple arithmetical problem, a problem of division: The dividend, *eternity,* over the divisor, *two choices*—heaven or hell—equals the quotient, *the unalterable destiny of your soul.*

$$\frac{\text{Eternity}}{\substack{\text{Choice}\\ \text{(Heaven or Hell)}}} = \substack{\text{Unalterable}\\ \text{Destiny}}$$

Are you really a Christian? You know how you can tell don't you? If you really belong to Christ, then right now, you can pray from your heart this prayer which concludes the canon of Scripture: "Even so, come, Lord Jesus." *Come quickly!*

CHAPTER 11

To Judge the Quick and the Dead

And I saw the dead, small and great, stand before God; and the books were opened: and another book was opened, which is the book of life: and the dead were judged out of those things which were written in the books, according to their works. . . . And whosoever was not found written in the book of life was cast into the lake of fire.

Revelation 20:12, 15

THE GREAT Daniel Webster was one of the most brilliant men in American history. When Secretary of State under President Fillmore, he once dined with twenty gentlemen at the Astor House in New York. On that occasion, he was strangely withdrawn and quite silent. To draw him out and into the conversation, one of the men said, "Mr. Secretary, would you tell us what is the most important thought that has ever occupied your mind?" Startled from his reverie, he looked around as if not quite sure just where he was, so far away were his thoughts from the occasion. Then he said, "You all know me. You are my friends. The most important thought that has ever occupied my mind is my individual responsibility to God."

He then discoursed on that subject for about twenty minutes. And having concluded, he arose from the table and retired to his room.

That is the theme to which I would like to call your attention: our individual responsibility to God. The Creed declares unequivocally, ". . . from thence He shall come to judge the

118

quick and the dead." There is a day which has been appointed in which God will judge the world. And to that end He has given us assurance that He has raised Christ from the dead.

As I write this, the attention of the nation has been drawn to two significant trials, one for manslaughter in south Florida, and another for aggravated rape in New England. We have seen the verdicts handed down: acquittal or condemnation. And we have seen how those who have received these verdicts were affected, after silently listening to their fate being read out. We have seen the rejoicing when one heard that he had been acquitted, and we have seen a head drop in weeping and sobbing when one heard that he had been condemned to life imprisonment.

But here I would call your attention to a far more solemn trial than those, a far more awesome spectacle than has been witnessed on this earth: *when God shall sit in judgment upon mankind.*

John the Apostle tells us that he saw "a great white throne, and him that sat upon it, from whose face the earth and the heaven fled away . . ." (Revelation 20:11). John saw a great white throne! ". . . It is appointed unto men," we are told, "once to die" (Hebrews 9:27) and then to stand before that throne in judgment.

A young minister, fresh out of seminary and hardly experienced at all, was accosted by a well-known skeptic named Burt Olney after a service one day. Olney said, "Young man, I don't believe in the infallibility of the Scriptures." The young man, not quite sure what to say, said, "Well, I don't know about all that. I *do* know that it is appointed unto men once to die, as my text declares, and then the judgment."

And Olney said, "But I can prove to you beyond any shadow of a doubt that there is no such thing as a final judgment." The minister said, "I am not here to debate the Scripture but simply to preach it, and my text declares plainly that it is appointed unto men once to die and then the judgment."

Getting somewhat exasperated, the skeptic said, "That is no argument. Now, let us sit down and debate the thing logically."

Again the reply, "I am not here to debate but simply to preach, and I tell you that the Scripture expressly declares that it is appointed unto men once to die and then the judgment."

Olney became so angry that he turned on his heel and stalked away. But as he was walking back to his home in the small country town, it seemed that the very tree toads and frogs in the river echoed the words: Judgment! Judgment! Judgment! And he could not shake from his mind that text which had been so indelibly impressed on his heart: "It is appointed unto men once to die, but after this the judgment."

He spent a sleepless night, and early the next morning there was a knock at the door of the parsonage of the young minister. There stood a white-faced ex-skeptic who said: "I could not get away from that text you kept repeating. And I want to know what must I do to be saved?

That day Burt Olney, the skeptic, became a believer, because he, too, had seen the great white throne.

Judgment Day Is Coming

The Bible unequivocally declares that there is coming a day of judgment, for God has appointed a day in which He will judge the world in righteousness. Jesus said that we will see the Son of Man sitting upon the throne of His glory, all nations will be gathered together before Him, and He will separate them as the shepherd separates the sheep from the goats.

John saw a great white throne in a great day of judgment. Not only does the Bible declare it, but also the moral nature of man demands it.

I remember one time seeing thanatologist Elizabeth Kübler-Ross when she appeared on the Phil Donahue program and was discussing her views of a future life. She is a universalist and believes that all men when they die go to heaven. As I recall, Donahue finally asked her, "Do you believe that Hitler went to heaven?" And she said, "Of course." There being a number of Jewish people in the audience that morning, they became quite agitated. They asked other questions about some of the various men who had headed up the Nazi death camps at Dachau and other places. She continued to affirm that all of these, too, upon their deaths, went immediately to paradise. By this time the audience had become so enraged that I thought some of them were going to rush upon her and gnash upon her with their teeth—because there is something in the moral nature of man that demands that wrongs will be righted and scores will be settled.

The Scripture speaks of the prosperity of the wicked. (In Psalm 73, one laments that he had cleansed his heart in vain because he saw the prosperity of the wicked and how the righteous often suffered.) But there is coming a day when righteousness will be rewarded and iniquity will be punished. As surely as there is a God in heaven, that day is coming when all things *will* be made right!

All of human history is flowing irresistibly toward that day of judgment, and all of the generations of men are moving ineluctably toward it, because all of the declarations of Scripture point unalterably toward that day of judgment, a day when God shall sit upon the throne. From that judgment there shall be no escape, from that verdict there shall be no appeal, and from that sentence there shall be no parole—when God sits in judgment upon that great white throne.

This will be the ultimate theodicy. (Theodicy is that which justifies the ways of God with men.) Many people have questions about things, but all of those questions will be answered in that great day. Keep in mind that the final judgment is not for God to grade the papers and find out how we did. God knew how we would do before He created the world. Known to Him are all things from the beginning of the creation. The judgment is for men to discover why God has done what He has done, and for men to realize that the judgment that they receive is altogether just and righteous. At that moment all appearances will be ripped away and reality will stand forth starkly.

Judged by Our Works

Men will be judged, not according to their profession, not according to their ecclesiastical connection, not according to their sacramental usage, but according to the reality of their hearts. The books will be opened and the dead and the living will be judged according to their works, we are told. But some people are confused as to why we should be judged according to our works. They ask, "Are we not saved by grace through faith?" Well, yes, of course, but the Bible makes it plain that, though salvation is according to faith, judgment in the Scripture is always by works.

Why is that? Very simply it is because faith is invisible and cannot be seen. As James says: "Show me thy faith without thy works, and I will show thee my faith by my works" (James 2:18). It is impossible for me to show my faith apart from my works. And since the purpose of the judgment is to show to all mankind why men are receiving what they receive, judgment is by works. Our works declare the reality of our faith and show us for what we really are.

In considering the judgment I do not want to divide our attention or confuse the issue with lesser questions, such as "when" or "where" or "how." Many of these questions are obscure, but the Creed focuses our attention on the great fact that the judgment will come. He will come to judge the quick and the dead.

The Judge and the Judged

Who is it that will be the judge? Recently I was in Dallas, Texas, where I was taxied in from the airport by a young black lady, who, during our conversation, revealed that she was a Muslim. In talking about Jesus Christ, she finally said that she didn't need a Savior; that she didn't need a redeemer; that, in fact, she would tell God what a good life she had led—how moral she was and how much good she had done. I said that I hoped that she realized that the God to whom she would be speaking would be none other than Jesus Himself.

For the Scripture declares that all judgment is given into the hands of the Son so that He may be equal with the Father. It is Christ who will come to judge the living and the dead. This One who knows us through and through, who is the altogether perfect man and God, the divine God-man, the *theanthropos,* will come to sit in judgment. He will be the judge. And who will be standing in the dock? Scripture makes it plain that *all mankind* will be judged—both the saved and the lost.

Christ said that He will separate the nations of the world, as the shepherd separates the sheep from the goats. Some people don't like the idea of separation. They would rather have everybody heaped into one big pile. They say, "After all, we are all the same." The Bible says, "Nay." The Scriptures inevitably cleave mankind in half: There are those that are the sheep, and there are those that are the goats; there is the wheat and there are the tares; there are the good fish and there are the bad; there are the saved and there are the lost; there are those who are on their way to heaven and there are those who are on their way to hell. And that separation will be manifest in that day.

On which side of that group will you be? All of the lost will be there. All of the skeptics and atheists and agnostics will be there. All of the unbelievers and those who have mocked at Christ, those who have taken His name in vain, and those who have laughed at the Bible will all be there then. Their eyes will not believe what they see. They will be astonished beyond measure; they, indeed, may look for some place to hide, but they will find no such place. Though they may call upon the mountains to cover them, the hills to hide them from the face of Him that sits upon the throne, they will find no such covering.

As they stand before the Lamb of God who now sits as judge of all of the world, all those guilty of blasphemy will be there, along with those whom we hear everywhere today taking the name of God in vain. They will wish that their tongues could fall out as they are forced to recall the innumerable blasphemies that were uttered by their lips. All of those who have profane mouths, who cannot seem to speak without using vile profanity—all of those will be there.

And all of those who are guilty of adultery and fornication and all manner of vile lusts and perversions will be there. All liars will be there to have their place in the lake that burns with fire, the Scripture says. Deceivers and cheaters and the dishonest will be there. All of those will be there. In addition to that, all of those who have professed faith in Jesus Christ when their profession was simply an empty word—they will be there! And they will not be judged on the basis of their profession, but on the basis of their heart. Those who have had their names on the roll of the church, and those who have been baptized will be there. There will even be those there whom I have baptized at the font in our church, and they will be there to hear the words of Jesus: "Depart from Me! I never knew you! ye workers of iniquity." For their professions have been but hypocrisy.

Throughout the week their lives have given the lie to all that they have professed on Sunday. They have lived for the world, the flesh, and the devil, and not for Jesus Christ. And in that day the reality of their profession, or should I say, the unreality of it, will be made manifest to all.

God's Standard

We should remember by what standard God judges. He does not grade on a bell curve as so many imagine. There are so many who say, "Well, yes, I know that I am a sinner, but I am better than many. I am not as bad as so and so." God grades on no curve at all! The passing grade is very clear: "Be ye, therefore, perfect . . ." (Matthew 5:48), said Christ. "Be ye, therefore, perfect, even as your Father which is in heaven is perfect."

God's standard is perfection in thought, word, and deed—in total obedience to His command, for if you offend in one point, you are guilty of all. "Cursed is every one that continueth not in all things which are written in the book of the law to do them" (Galatians 3:10).

At the judgment there will also be those who have supposed that they can trust in their own goodness, who have supposed that they have not committed many heinous crimes—who have supposed that they are not guilty of breaking the laws of men. They have been respectable in their communities, and they will tell God how good they have been. All of those will be there to hear the dire sentence of Christ: "Depart from me, ye workers of iniquity," for unless we come to the Savior Himself, there is no hope. Since God's standard is perfection and since we all have come short of that glory, every one of us is in desperate need of a redeemer. "Whosoever was not found written in the book of life was cast into the lake of fire" (Revelation 20:15). Has your name been written in that Book? Have you trusted in Jesus Christ as your Savior and Lord? If not, then you will hear that awful sentence of doom: "Depart from me. I never knew you."

Also gathered there will be all of the saints of history: all of those who have believed in the Savior, from the Old Testament days until the last day. From all nations, tongues, and tribes throughout the earth, there shall be gathered together a vast host—whom no man can number—of men and women who have trusted in the redemption of Jesus Christ. And they shall receive their rewards!

Remember that just as there are degrees of punishment in hell, so there are degrees of reward in heaven. As it is true that God says of the lost that it shall be more tolerable for some than others, and that some shall receive the "greater condemnation," so also in heaven there will be different rewards because of our faithfulness. We get into heaven by receiving Christ as our Savior and Lord. But even then God is willing, on top of that and by His grace, to give us rewards. And those rewards are of grace since the best works of the best of God's saints cannot deserve any reward. Many will suffer loss—even those who truly believe—because they have not faithfully served Christ.

Obedience to the Great Commission

How will it be for you? Will you come before Him and be unable to name even one soul saved because of your influence? How will it be? How obedient have you been to the great commission which Jesus Christ gave: "Ye shall be witnesses unto me." "Go and preach the gospel to every creature."

Some Christians have remained in craven silence throughout these years. Some must come before Him without one soul—one other person—who has come to know Christ because of you. What a tragedy that is! Dear friend, are you a faithful witness for Jesus Christ? Not only by your life, but also by your lips? Do you serve Christ and His church? You took a vow that you would serve Christ to the best of your ability in His church, and yet have you ever given one day, or even one hour, to the service of Christ? You are never to be found in church on Sunday evening or at prayer meeting. You are never to be found in any hour of service. When all of the appeals are made, they all go right over your head. You offer no service for Christ.

Ah, I even wonder if you are really saved at all. Some do not make it a habit to read God's Word or to seek Him faithfully in prayer. Others do not bring their tithes and offerings to Christ. Instead, like Demas, you have loved this present world. All of these things will come out at the judgment. And how will it be for you in that day?

The Judgment

Then, finally, there is the sentence and judgment itself. On the one hand Christ will say: "Depart from me, for I never knew you." And they will go out into the second death. They will be cast into the lake of fire. This is the second death. The Bible makes it very clear: Born once; die twice. Born twice; die once. There is a second birth and there is a second death. And only those who have experienced the second birth shall not experience the second death.

Have you experienced that new birth which only Christ can give? If not, then there awaits you naught but the second death. On the other hand, there is the word of the Savior: "Come ye blessed of my Father, inherit the kingdom prepared for you from the foundation of the world" (Matthew 25:34). And we shall go to that place which Jesus has prepared for us, which eye has not seen nor ear heard, which never entered into the heart of man, that God has prepared for them that love Him.

And we shall see paradise itself. Beyond anything we have ever thought or said, we shall see God in all of His glory. What a marvelous day that will be!

There is coming, my friends, a day of judgment and a day of separation. How will it be for you in that day? In that day of judgment, do you realize that you would give everything you own for an opportunity to accept Christ as your Savior? But by then, the day of grace will irrevocably have closed and the day of judgment will have come. You would give all that you own and you would give all of the wealth of this world or ten thousand worlds for simply one minute—for simply one second— in which to reach out and take hold of the grace of God.

Moments unnumbered have gone before: You have heard the gracious invitation of Christ: "Come unto me, all ye that labor and are heavy laden, and I will give you rest" (Matthew 11:28).

You have heard the offer of forgiveness for all of your sins: "Though your sins be as scarlet, they shall be white as snow . . ." (Isaiah 1:18). You have heard that you can come to the cross and receive Jesus Christ as your own personal Redeemer. You can receive the gift of eternal life; you can receive your title deed to paradise by simple faith in Christ and repentance for your sins. You have heard that over and over and over again, but you have spurned it every time. But in that day, in that great day, you would give all that exists in all of the universe for one more moment to receive it. And, my friend, that moment will never, ever, come. It will be everlastingly too late! Eternity will have dawned. Everlasting, never-ending life in the bliss and felicity of paradise or the pain and condign punishment of hell. What an awesome day that will be when the day of judgment replaces the day of grace.

But, dear friend, the sun of righteousness is still in the heavens above, and the day of grace still shines upon you. It could end this very day. You have that moment now. If you have never received Him, if you have never surrendered your life to Christ, if you have never enthroned Him as Lord and Master of your heart, I urge you, I beseech you, as Paul did, "be ye reconciled unto God." Won't you do that now? Look to Him, for, my friend, "it is appointed unto men once to die, but then the judgment." "And whosoever was not found written in the book of life was cast into the lake of fire."

CHAPTER 12

The Holy Ghost

"Jesus answered, Verily, verily, I say unto thee, Except a man be born of water and of the Spirit, he cannot enter into the kingdom of God."

John 3:5

I ONCE saw a great machine that filled almost a whole huge room. It was moving mightily with thousands of parts whirling and turning out its product. But all of a sudden it stopped! People began to scurry about, trying to fix it. The problem? Very simple. Someone had disconnected the power source and all of that massive machinery was of no more use than a pile of junk. And so it is with our Christian lives: Unless we have the power of God, then all that we know and all that we have learned will mean nothing. Our lives will be impotent, filled with discord and strife, instead of the joy and peace and love of Christ. These come with the power, and power comes from the Holy Spirit.

In this chapter we deal with that portion of the Apostles' Creed which states: "I believe in the Holy Ghost."

I have discovered from a personal survey that a large percentage of the people of America are confused as to just who Jesus Christ is. They think Him to be a great teacher, a great example, our marvelous exemplar; but only a minority of those surveyed understood that He was, indeed, God incarnate. If there is confusion concerning who Jesus Christ is, there is even more confusion concerning the Holy Ghost. The very words themselves cause many people to wonder: Did we not learn as children not to believe in ghosts? A ghost! Isn't that an apparition of the departed dead? And yet we are talking here about a living, vivifying spirit. Of course, "ghost" is simply an old English word for "spirit." They are synonymous.

Some of the old English books on the Christian life talk about sanctification and speak of improving your "ghostly" life. I am sure that today, if somebody saw a book on how to improve your ghostly life, they would think it was something out of the occult. The books were talking, of course, about our spiritual life. "I believe in the Holy Ghost," or the Holy Spirit.

Aspects of the Holy Spirit

Let's think about the Holy Spirit by trying to answer three questions: Who is He? What does He do? How may we experience the blessing of the Holy Spirit?

First of all: Who is He? Or should I say "What is it?" I have noticed that a number of people, when referring to the Holy Spirit, refer to an "it." That is not surprising, seeing that virtually all of the cults deny that the Holy Spirit is a personality, a person. They all declare that He is an "it." This is most vociferously maintained by Jehovah's Witnesses, for example, or Christian Scientists, or Unitarians. They all agree in denying that the Holy Spirit is a person. Some of them will boldly say, "Show me in the Scripture where it says that the Holy Spirit is a person."

Shall I show where it says that the Holy Spirit is a person? It says it nowhere at all! But before the cultists become too ecstatic over that, let me also mention that nowhere does it say in the Bible that the Father is a person. You may look in vain for any statement that says that the Father is a person. And yet, the attributes of personality are everywhere ascribed to the Father.

The same thing is true of the Holy Spirit. All of the attributes of personality are ascribed to the Holy Spirit. For example: intellect, emotion, volition, mind, heart, and will, and along with these, the ability to communicate and to act.

The Bible refers to the *mind* of the Spirit. If the Holy Spirit is merely a force, as the cultists maintain, if He were no different, as they say, from such forces as gravity or magnetism or electricity, then how could we possibly speak of the mind of the Spirit. Did you ever hear of the mind of gravity? The idea is absurd!

Furthermore, the Scripture says that the Holy Spirit knows with His mind. In fact, it says that no one knows the deep things of God except the Spirit of God. Not only does the Spirit of God know, but He also foreknows the future. The Bible tells us that the Spirit will tell us of things that will come to pass. So the Holy Spirit evidently has intellect and mind.

What about emotion? The Bible says that we are not to grieve the Spirit of God. Did you ever hear of magnetism or gravity grieving? The idea is ludicrous! Furthermore, the Bible speaks of "the love of the Spirit." Now, if the Spirit has love and the Spirit can be grieved, then the Spirit obviously has emotional qualities.

How about volition or will? The Holy Spirit said, "Separate me Barnabas and Saul for the work whereunto I have called them" (Acts 13:2). The Holy Spirit *willed* that Barnabas and Saul should be set apart for the work to which He had called them. The Holy Spirit forbade them to go into Asia. Rather He led them on another course. The Holy Spirit clearly has volition, will, and therefore He can act. And He does in many ways, as we shall see.

Furthermore, it is obvious that with these attributes the Holy Spirit communicates. He takes the things of Christ and tells them to us—reveals them to us. The Holy Spirit speaks and hears. The Holy Spirit, therefore, has all the attributes of a person; the Holy Spirit *is* a person. Of that there can be no reasonable doubt.

What kind of a person then is this Holy Spirit? The Bible makes it plain that He is a divine person. Again the cultists will rise up and demand, "Where does it say that the Holy Spirit is God?" In Acts, chapter 5, when Peter is speaking to Ananias and Sapphira, who withheld a portion of that which they claimed to have given to the Lord, Peter says: "Why hath

Satan filled thine heart to lie to the Holy Ghost?" (v.3). And then he says, "Thou hast not lied unto men, but unto God" (v.4). To lie to the Holy Ghost is to lie to God.

Therefore, it is clearly seen in Scripture that the Holy Spirit is God. He is a person, the third person of the triune Godhead. We might note that in the Apostles' Creed there are three paragraphs: The first paragraph deals with the Father ("I believe in God, the Father Almighty, maker of heaven and earth.") The second deals with the Son (*and* in Jesus Christ His only Son, our Lord.") The third begins with an affirmation of our belief in the Holy Spirit ("I believe in the Holy Ghost.") And so we see that the Apostles' Creed is a trinitarian formulation, just as all Christian worship is trinitarian. We talk about the *Gloria Patri,* the doxology: "Glory be to the Father, and to the Son, and to the Holy Ghost." Or:

> Praise God, from whom all blessings flow;
> Praise Him, all creatures here below;
> Praise Him above, ye heavenly host;
> Praise Father, Son, and Holy Ghost.

Praise who? Father, Son and *Holy Ghost.* The entirety of Christian worship is built on the concept of the triune God: Father, Son, and Holy Spirit.

What Does He Do?

His works are manifold indeed. To begin with, there is credited to His work the creation of our world. Remember that the world was without form and void until the Holy Spirit, the Spirit of God, brooded upon this waste and transformed that chaos into cosmos, into an orderly system, into the beautiful world which we see today.

Furthermore, we see that the Holy Spirit is responsible for giving us the Scriptures. "All scripture is given by inspiration of God" (2 Timothy 3:16). It is given by the Holy Spirit. The Holy Spirit has caused the Apostles and the Prophets to write those things which God would have us receive, so that we may know that these are the words which God has given—having been inspired by the Holy Spirit of God in a unique way in which nothing else has ever been inspired. As John Calvin said, "We may receive the words of the Holy Scriptures as if they dripped from the very lips of God."

Thirdly, the Holy Spirit was responsible for bringing Christ into the world. The Spirit came upon Mary and caused Jesus Christ to be conceived in her womb.

Fourthly, notice that at Pentecost the Holy Spirit brought into existence the Christian church. We see that the Holy Spirit is responsible for the creation of the world, of the Scriptures, of the incarnation of Jesus Christ, and also of the Church. These, indeed, are mighty works which are attributed in Scripture to the Holy Spirit.

Furthermore, there are other works which the Holy Spirit does personally in our lives: The Holy Spirit is responsible for regeneration; that is, we must be born of the Spirit. Jesus Christ said, "Ye must be born again." Except we have been born of the Spirit, we shall in no wise enter the Kingdom of God (see John 3:5, 7).

How tragic it is that so many millions of people in this country have been satisfied merely to have their names on a church roll, and to be baptized or confirmed. Yet they have never experienced the transforming, regenerating power of the Holy Spirit, which alone can make them acceptable for admission into heaven. It is only when we repent of our sins and receive Christ as Lord and Savior of our lives that we are renewed by the Holy Spirit of God.

The Holy Spirit is not only the regenerator of men, but He is also the sanctifier as well. There are many emblems in the Scripture of the Holy Spirit: the dove of peace as the Spirit brings, the peace of God which passeth understanding; the emblem of water as we are washed by the Holy Spirit; the emblem of wind as the Holy Spirit blows and renews and cleanses; and the symbol of fire as the cloven tongues of fire sat upon the disciples at Pentecost. The Spirit purifies us. If we are ever to see God, we must have a pure heart, the Bible tells us. There is so much sin in the best of us—so much iniquity in all of us—that we need the purging, purifying power of the Holy Spirit to cleanse us in our lives.

In 1665, the Great Plague had London in its grip. And everywhere throughout the city, people were filled with panic and fear. The germs continued to spread unabated, hiding in all sorts of dark corners, only to break out and destroy more and more lives. Then suddenly and unexpectedly London caught fire, and the fire spread until the entire city was consumed in a great conflagration. Though the buildings were destroyed, the raging fire brought an end to the plague—the unclean germs were purged by the fire.

And so it is in our life. The fire of the Spirit needs to purge our hearts of sin. Only the Holy Spirit can take away all of the dregs of sin in our own life and cleanse us—from lascivious thoughts, from evil deeds, from lust and impurity, from lying and cheating, from hostility and animosity, from envy and jealousy, and from rancor and bickering and strife. Only the Spirit of God can take these things away. We need for the Spirit to cleanse and purge our lives. We need to call upon God daily to have that work done.

Further, the Spirit of God is the One who brings power to our lives. He is the Spirit of power, the Scripture tells us. How we need that power in our lives! How many Christians seem impotent to serve God, impotent to witness effectively for Christ? How many have never brought another living soul to Christ?

One minister was sitting on a trolley car years ago and he noticed that when the motorman moved the handle a little bit, the car would start slowly forward. When he moved it more, it would go more rapidly. That would be easily understood if the trolley were powered by a gasoline engine. But he thought that with electrical power, all of that energy should surge the engine, driving the trolley car at full speed the moment the trolley came in contact with the wire. There is no halfway in between. Likewise with a light.

So he asked the motorman about it. In reply the motorman

said, "When I push this, the gripper grips the wire, but it does it ever so gently and only a little of the power flows into the machine. But when it grips it tightly, then the full power flows into the trolley car and it goes faster." He said, "We call the gentle grip 'skinning the wire.' "

The minister thought, *I have got several thousand members in my congregation who are just "skinning the wire." They just barely have enough power to inch along in their Christian lives. And they never accomplish anything for Jesus Christ.*

My friend, what have you accomplished for Christ? You may be moving toward the end of your life but what have you accomplished for Christ? Is there one living person that today is alive in Christ because of you?

The Holy Spirit also gives us fruit of the Spirit: love, joy, peace, longsuffering, gentleness, goodness, faith, meekness, and temperance (*see* Galatians 5:22, 23). That fruit only comes from the Spirit of God.

How is it in your heart? How is it in your home? If there is love and joy and peace, then the Spirit of God is filling you. But if there is bitterness, rancor and strife, hostility and envy, then the Spirit of God is not there. How we all need to see the Spirit of God flowing through us and producing that beautiful cluster of fruit in our lives!

The Spirit of God also is the One who gives us assurance. It is by the Spirit of God that we know our adoption. By the Spirit of God we know we belong to Him. By the Spirit of God we can say "Abba, Father." It is the Spirit that witnesses to our spirit that we are the children of God. Do you have that assurance in your heart today?

It is the Spirit of God who also guides our lives and leads us. The Scripture says, "For as many as are led by the Spirit of God, they are the sons of God" (Romans 8:14). How wonderful it is to know that there is someone who is willing to lead our lives! So many times we don't know what to do or where to go or which way to turn. When we yield ourselves to the Holy Spirit, He has promised to lead us.

You can go off on a trip to Europe somewhere and try to

make it on your own. You may not speak the various languages; you may not have reservations when you get there; you
may not know how to get to the train station; you may not
know when your next flight is taking place; and you may be
very confused. Or you can engage a good travel agent to lay
out the entire itinerary for you. Then you will know that, wherever you go, your hotel has been planned, your flight has been
planned, and your train has been planned. Everything has
been arranged.

So it is with the Holy Spirit. We can commit our lives to
Him, and He will plan our itinerary through this world. Some
Christians are blindly staggering around, knowing not where
they are going; they have never, by faith, committed their lives
to the Holy Spirit. "As many as are led by the Spirit of God,
they are the sons of God" (Romans 8:14).

Finally, the Holy Spirit testifies of Jesus Christ. Jesus said
that when the Spirit of truth shall come He will not speak of
Himself, but He will testify of Christ.

Dr. Manford Gutzke used to say this: "You can always tell a
church or an individual that is filled with the Spirit of God.
How? Because of the fact that he is speaking or that church is
speaking much about Jesus Christ." And he added that you
can always know that if a church or an individual is speaking
all of the time about the Holy Spirit, then that person or
church is not energized and motivated by the Holy Spirit of
God. For the Holy Spirit speaks not of Himself but testifies "of
Me," said Jesus (*see* John 15:26; 16:13).

What Are His Blessings?

The Bible says, "Be filled with the Holy Spirit." "Be not
drunk with wine wherein is excess; but be ye filled with the
Spirit," (Ephesians 5:18). I have in the past used an illustration
such as this: We are leaky vessels, like sieves. Though we may
be filled, we leak out that power. We need to be refilled. But I
have come to see that that is not really the best analogy for
being filled with the Holy Spirit, because the Holy Spirit is a
person and you cannot have part of a person in you

and have part of that person leak out of you. That is not the case at all.

I think a better illustration is this: Suppose you have a house without air conditioning, and so your house is hot inside, stuffy and musty and moldy and mildewed. It is just miserable to live there! So you break down and buy an air conditioner, a wall unit which you place in the central room in your house. Then cool air flows into that room: it flows through the doorways and into all of the other rooms. It cools your entire house, assuming the unit is adequate for the job. Everything is delightful!

But then you begin to close the doors in one room after another. And you leave them closed. The first thing you know you have only one room that is cool and all of the rest of the house is hot and stuffy and mildewed again. Miserable!

That is the way it is with the Spirit of God. It is not that we need more of the Spirit; it is that the Holy Spirit wants more of us. It is that we have confined Him in one small room of our lives and there are parts of our lives that we are witholding from Him. We need to throw open the doors and let the Holy Spirit take over our minds, our habits, our hearts, our affections, our will, our speech, our feet, our hands, and all else that we are—and then let the Holy Spirit have control of all of our lives. This is what we need if we would be filled with the Holy Spirit and have every part of our being know the power and joy of the Holy Spirit. How can that be done?

First we must *confess* our sins, the Scripture says. All of the sins! Confess all of the doors that have been closed to Him in all of the areas of our life: our marriage relationship; our relationship with our parents, our children, and our friends; our relationships in our business, including our honesty and our personal relationships; our sex lives. Whatever the problem may be, we need to confess that sin.

We need, secondly, to *repent* of it—to determine by the grace of God to turn from that sin and follow Christ.

Thirdly, we need to *ask God* to fill us with the Holy Spirit. Jesus said, "If ye then, being evil, know how to give good gifts unto your children, how much more shall your Father which is in heaven give good things to them that ask him?" (Matthew 7:11). We need to ask God to fill us with the Holy Spirit. We are not asking Him to send the Holy Spirit if we are already a Christian, but rather to fill every part of our being with Him.

Fourthly, we need to *believe* that God will do just what Christ said—that the Father *will* give the Holy Spirit to them that ask Him. We don't need to wait for some ecstatic experience from God. It is the same as when we accept Christ: We must place our trust in Jesus Christ and take His word: "He that believeth in me already has eternal life." We believe His promise and we go out and live by that promise. The same thing is true with the Holy Spirit. We need to believe that God has filled us with His Spirit when we have asked Him after having confessed and repented of our sins.

Fifthly, and lastly, we need then to go out and *live,* knowing that we are empowered by the Spirit to go out and serve Christ. We are not given the Spirit merely for our own enjoyment or ecstasy, but that we might be servants of Christ and that we might glorify His name and build His Kingdom on the earth. Knowing that we have that power, we then need to go and live with that power, exercise that power, and thus be a faithful witness for Jesus Christ and serve Him through His church.

Dear friend, may Christ grant you that fullness of His Spirit as you seek it from Him, and may you determine this very day that you are not going to live just "skinning the wire," but that you are going to seek the fullness and power, the love and joy and peace that only the Holy Ghost can give you, so that you can say, in truth, from the very bottom of your heart: "I believe in the Holy Ghost!"

CHAPTER 13

The Holy Catholic Church

"And there came unto me one of the seven angels which had the seven vials full of the seven last plagues, and talked with me, saying, Come hither, I will show thee the bride, the Lamb's wife."

Revelation 21:9

A little boy was busily engaged in building something out in the backyard. And his father, observing the activity, went out to discover what was taking place. He said, "What are you building, son?" His boy said, "Sh, sh, I am building a church. We must be very quiet." His father, eager to encourage this sense of reverence in his son, said, "Just why must we be so quiet in church, son?" The little boy looked up, astonished that his father did not know, and said, "Because all of the people are asleep."

Well, the Puritans in New England knew how to deal with that: The ushers had a special implement for sleepers. It was a very long stick or pole that had affixed to one end a long and very sharp needle. And should anybody be observed to be sleeping in church, the usher would creep up behind, very stealthily, very silently, and suddenly, unexpectedly, he would take that needle and jab the sleeper. They knew how to wake up a sleepy congregation.

I think John Wesley had the best way of all. He was preaching the gospel mightily one day when he looked down and there, right in front of the pulpit, was a man snoozing away—sound asleep, sawing logs. Right in the middle of the sentence Wesley stopped, and a silence engulfed the room. In the midst of that silence, Wesley cried out: "Fire! Fire!" And the man leaped to his feet in surprise and said, "Where? Where?" Wesley shouted in reply, "In hell, man, for those who sleep under the gospel."

I think that of all of the statistics I have heard the one I like best is about sleepers in church. It has been authoritatively computed that if you were to take all of the people in America that go to sleep in church on any given Sunday and if you were to stretch them all out end-to-end, they would be a lot more comfortable! (In our church we have thought about putting in recliners, but we wouldn't want to make it too easy.)

There are those who sleep in church, but there are also those who just sleep in bed rather than even bother getting up and coming at all. They have all sorts of excuses about why they don't come to church: They are too sleepy or they have some other problems.

The Lutheran minister who listed in his bulletin some of the excuses which people give put it very well. And I think it shows something of the hypocrisy involved in most of the excuses that are given. He said: *I don't go to the movies because:*

1. My parents made me go when I was a child.
2. No one speaks to me when I am there.
3. Because they always ask for money.
4. Because the manager never visits me at home.
5. Because the people who do go don't live according to what the movies teach.

I am not sure about that last one anymore!

But in spite of all the criticism, the church has continued to grow. Jesus Christ guarantees that the gates of hell would not prevail against it. He said He would build His church—build it upon that profession that Peter had made—"Thou art the Christ, the Son of the living God" (Matthew 16:16). And wherever anyone, from his heart, comes to profess and confess and believe that Jesus Christ is the Divine Redeemer and trusts in Him as his Savior and Lord, the church of Jesus Christ is built and continues to grow.

Some people have tried to minimize the church. Certainly our secularized media today does not even recognize that the church exists. In fact, there is as we heard recently not a single Christian portrayed in any contemporary television program on the air today. You would suppose that the church became a complete fossil a few decades ago, that it ceased to exist, or that it is no longer extant in our world.

Yet you need to remember that if you took all of the people who attend professional sports games all year long—including football, baseball, basketball, hockey, and soccer—all of them!—and add them all up, the grand total does not even come close to the numbers of people who attend church in any given year in America.

The church is the most important institution in the history of the world. It is the largest institution that has ever existed upon the face of this planet. Today there are over 1,350,000,000 people who profess their faith in Jesus Christ. By the end of the next century it is estimated that at the present rate of growth there will be approximately 5 billion members in the Christian church. Within the last five years, the church outstripped the world in its rate of growth, in spite of the tremendous rate of growth of the world population.

The Church Visible and Invisible

Now we come to that segment of the Apostles' Creed which declares: "I believe in the holy catholic church." What does that mean? It is a phrase which has confused many. *I believe in the church,* says the Creed. Not merely in Christ, but also the church which is His body. Not simply in churches, with a small *c,* but in the Church, with a capital *C.* The Church of Jesus Christ, the universal church of Christ.

The Westminster Confession of Faith says that "the universal Church, which is invisible, consists of the whole number of the elect, that have been, are, or shall be gathered together into one, under Christ the head thereof; and is the spouse, the body, the fullness of Him that filleth all in all" (*see* Ephesians 1:22, 23). The church is those things.

There is a church visible and a church invisible. The *visible* church of Christ can be seen by any passerby or any who would come in to observe it. It consists of all those who have made a profession of their faith in Jesus Christ. But the Bible would have us to know that this is not the real church of Christ. The real church of Christ is *invisible*. It consists of all those who truly belong to God, all of God's elect, all those who have been regenerated by the Holy Spirit (in ages past, in the present, and in the ages to come)—all whose hearts have been transformed by Christ and consequently have been born anew.

Some people suppose that the "born-again" Christian is a new phenomenon. Some people suppose that it is almost a new denomination. But, my friend, there is no other kind of real Christian except those who have been born anew—those who have been regenerated from above. Jesus said it is necessary for us to be born again, and if we are not, we can in no wise enter into the kingdom of heaven. Down through the centuries, every branch of the church of Christ has always agreed that unless a person is born of the Spirit of God, unless he has been born again, he can in no wise enter the kingdom of heaven. That is the invisible church.

I would ask you: Are you a part of that church? Yes? Your name may be on the roll. Yes? You may have been baptized. Yes? You may partake of the sacrament of the Lord's Supper. Yes? But are you a part of the invisible church of Christ? Is your name written in the Lamb's Book of Life? That is the question! Have you been born anew? Do not be satisifed with the mere externalities of religion. Religion is a matter of the heart, a transformation of the soul that only the Spirit of God can bring about.

I assure you that the fact that your name is written on the roll of some church will not at all suffice when you stand before that great assize and the judgment commences. The question then will be, "Is your name in the Lamb's Book of Life?" All of those whose names are not found written in the Lamb's Book of Life will be cast into the lake of fire. Are you a member of the invisible church of Jesus Christ? That is the ultimate question!

The Church Militant and Triumphant

The church is also divided, not only into the visible and invisible aspects of it, but also into the church militant and the church triumphant. We are a part of the church militant here, the church which is called to a good warfare to follow Christ, her captain in the well-fought fight. We are engaged in a great struggle. "Like a mighty army moves the church of God," the hymn writer put it.

The church triumphant is composed of those who have passed through the warfare and have entered into the glory above. But now we are engaged in that struggle. We are called to be good soldiers of Jesus Christ, to fight the good fight with the sword of the Spirit, and to take the gospel of Christ to every person upon this planet.

I would ask you: Are you a soldier of Christ? Are you engaged in that warfare? The sword with which we fight is the gospel of Christ, the Word of God. Have you been engaged in battle in this past week? Have you used that sword for the glory of Christ? With that sword we do not kill, but we make alive from the dead.

Or have you been AWOL, absent without leave, as so many are who profess to be a part of the church of Christ? One of the ways that you can tell if you are part of the real, invisible church is by whether or not you are a soldier of Christ, whether you are concerned with that which concerns the heart of Christ, whether the master passion of the Master is the master passion of your soul, whether you are concerned for lost men and women. This is the great task which Christ has given to His church: to take the good tidings of Christ to a perishing world. "I believe in the church of Jesus Christ."

I have received a number of honors in my lifetime and I am a member of numerous organizations. In fact, someone told me recently that it took three pages to list the organizations of which I am a board member. But of all of those organizations and honors, the greatest organization and the greatest honor which has ever come into my life is being a part of the church of Jesus Christ. Nothing in this world even vaguely approaches it. "I believe in the church of Jesus Christ."

The Holy Catholic Church

"I believe in the holy catholic church," we confess. Now, some people are confused about why Presbyterians or Lutherans or Methodists or whatever are confessing their belief in the catholic church. This is because of a confusion over semantics. The word *catholic* comes from the two Greek words, *cata,* "according to," and *holos,* "the whole"—according to the whole, or, universal. It simply means that we believe in a holy universal church, a church which is broader than the boundaries of our own parochial denomination.

There are some Christians who suppose that the church is no broader than their own denomination and who are going to be utterly amazed to find people from other denominations in heaven. But we believe that there is a universal church that consists of all of God's elect—everywhere in every communion—who have trusted in Jesus Christ, who have repented of their sins, and who have received Him as Lord and Savior, regardless of what denominational label they may have on their back. They are a part of the universal or catholic church of Jesus Christ.

Four hundred years ago, Dr. Francis Junius of the University of Holland described that catholic or universal church in this way: "The holy catholic church is the congregation of them all, who by the election of God are called together in Christ Jesus to eternal life." All of them throughout the ages past, all the way back to Adam, and throughout all the ages that may come in the future, all of those that have been gathered unto Jesus Christ—all are part of that holy catholic or universal church.

It is a holy church as well—holy because it calls out of the world, to be set aside unto God. The word *holy* has two meanings in Scripture: It means "set aside unto the worship and service of God." And that is what the church is, called away from the world, even as the word *temple* comes from the root "to cut," bearing reference to the groove cut in the ground marking where a temple was to be built. It was separated unto God. And so the church is separated unto God.

Secondly, the word means "to cleanse," "to purify." And those who are part of the invisible church of God, who are truly God's own, find that their hearts have been sanctified and cleansed. They are daily becoming more and more clean as they are being prepared for that day when there shall be no spot or wrinkle or any such thing. Then we shall be a perfect, holy church in heaven. The church is a long way from being perfect today; it is always in the process of being cleansed. For in the visible church there are both the sheep and the goats.

Now the goat is one of the most unclean of animals. When I was in Israel one time I learned that there is a simple way to tell the sheep from the goats. As we were watching the shepherds with their herds, our guide pointed out to me that the goats were in front of the shepherd while the sheep were following behind. He said, "Note carefully! See how the sheep follow the shepherd, but the goats he has to drive with a stick!" And so it is with the church. The sheep follow the shepherd. But those goats! Sometime I think that there isn't a stick big enough to drive some of the goats. Do you follow gladly? Willingly? Joyfully? Or must you be driven? That is one indication of whether you're a sheep or a goat.

The holy catholic church has been mightily used for good in this world. It brought about the end of the greatest plague upon antiquity: slavery. Half of the Roman world was enmeshed in slavery until Christianity came and destroyed the bonds of slavery. But it was reinstituted in 1516, a year before Luther nailed the ninety-five theses to the church door in Wittenberg. Again it was a Christian, this time William Wilberforce (converted by Wesley), who devoted his life to the abolition of slavery in England. And it was from the pulpits of the churches that slavery finally was destroyed by the thundering pronouncements of the Word of God.

Receive him not as a servant, said Paul to Philemon but as a brother. Those simple words bore the seed of slavery's destruction from the ancient and modern world.

It was the church of Christ that did away with the ghastly practice of infanticide in the ancient pagan world. Before then children were left out on mountainsides to be consumed by wild beasts or by those perverted creatures that crept around in the night and gathered them up for even more horrible fates.

It was Christianity that did away with the gladiatorial fights, part of that terrible system where hundreds of thousands of people gave their lives yearly to satisfy the blood lust of the Romans. The system ended abruptly after Telemachus, a Christian, jumped into the arena and pushed aside two gladiators, who then plunged their swords into him. The people, seeing that holy man lying there in his blood, were so shocked that they arose in silence and walked out of the arena, never again to return for the gladiatorial fights.

It was the church of Christ proclaiming the gospel that freed women from the tremendous enslavement that they always have endured in pagan lands. I have seen, in a pagan culture, a woman yoked together with an ox pulling a plow in a field. It was Christ, through His church, who lifted up women. When Jesus took a little child into His arms and blessed him, children then assumed the dignity that they had never known before.

It was Christ, through His church and His missionaries, who took away the tremendous evil of cannibalism and head-hunting. Captain Cook and his men tell the story of landing on an island they would later call Cannibal Island. Two boats were sent ashore and the sailors began to explore the island to see what they could find. Suddenly, what seemed like hundreds of screaming natives raced toward them. The sailors fled, jumping into their boats amid a flurry of arrows and spears, and put out to sea. But one man was hit and lay wounded on the beach. In vain he reached out his hands toward his mates who fled to the safety of the ship. From there they watched in horror as the natives cooked their shipmate and ate him.

Twenty years later, sailing again in those same waters, Cook and his ship went aground on the rocks. A number of men were saved in a lifeboat and as they made for shore the captain realized that they were again approaching Cannibal Island. He ordered his men to pull hard at the oars to take them away from that island, knowing what fate awaited them. But the waves were too great. They continued to be swept toward the shore until finally the lifeboat itself was smashed to pieces on the rocks. The men dragged themselves onto the island. One of them crept up the hill, moved the grass apart, and looked inland, his heart pounding within him. But then he leaped to his feet and shouted: "We're safe. We're safe. I see a steeple and a cross." The missionary had arrived with his magic wand, the wand of the gospel, and that island had been transformed.

Its Diversity

Some people suppose that there are different churches and all believe different things. But let us remember: "In essentials, unity; in nonessentials, liberty; and in all things, charity." And so it is! The church exists in many different folds, but it is one flock; there is one holy catholic church which consists of all of those who belong to Christ. Some people, indeed, lament the various denominations that exist in the world today. But, from another point of view, we might note that in America, with this great diversity of denominations, people attend church in much greater numbers than in any nation in Europe which has a state church. God uses the various diversities and differences in these denominations to enrich the church of Christ. Schism is not so much a matter of denominational organization as it is an attitude of the heart—an attitude of divisiveness, of scorn toward others, of superiority, and a desire to keep one's self away from others.

No. The holy catholic church of Jesus Christ, which is one, is composed of *all* our brothers and sisters in Jesus Christ. All true believers in whatever church are our brothers and sisters.

The Bible says that there will be one fold and one shepherd. At least the King James says that. But that is an improper translation. The word is not *aule,* "fold," but *poimne,* "flock." There will be one flock and one shepherd. Jesus said, "Other sheep I have which are not of this fold (*aule*) . . ." (John 10:16). There are different folds, but there is one flock and one shepherd.

In that diversity is a richness. Just think of the various aspects of the church of Christ, the various hues in the rainbow that are given by different churches: the Lutheran church, with its great emphasis upon the doctrine of justification by faith; the Methodist church, with its pioneer missionaries going out to the frontiers of America, taking the gospel and seeking the transformation of the hearts of men and women. (While the Presbyterians were putting their preachers through forty-two years of college, the Methodists were out winning the frontier for Christ!) The Friends, with their quiet, reverent approach to God. The Baptists, with their tremendous evangelistic and missionary zeal. The Roman Catholic Church, with its emphasis upon the unity and historicity of the church. The Pentecostals, with their zeal and their hunger for God. The Anglicans with their elevated form of worship and the dignity and beauty of their service. All of these and more have added immeasurably to the richness of the diversity of the church of Jesus Christ. "I believe in the holy catholic church of Jesus Christ."

Its Purpose

I believe it has the greatest purpose in all of the world. It is the only agency in the world whose purpose is to bring about the salvation of mankind. That is the great purpose of the church: "Go into all the world and be witnesses unto me. Preach the gospel to every creature," said Jesus Christ (*see* Mark 16:15).

Is that the purpose of your life? Is the great burning passion of your heart to take the gospel to the lost? Recently I talked to a man who was quite irate because I had said that it is only through Christ that we may be saved. But Jesus Himself made it absolutely explicit: "I am *the* way, *the* truth and *the* life: no man cometh unto the Father but by me." (John 14:6 *italics added*). "There is none other name under heaven given among men whereby we must be saved" (Acts 4:12). The gospel of Christ is the power of God unto salvation. I am not ashamed to proclaim that Christ, the eternal second person of the trinity, the Creator of the universe, is the only hope of salvation that men have. And I don't care whether they gnash their teeth or whether they pound their fists or what they do—the truth cannot be changed. Christ is the way and the only way to the Father. He that has not the Son has not the Father. There is a great imperious tone to the gospel. It is only through Christ that we can be saved.

I was reading recently of an engineer on a local passenger train who had pulled his train off the main track to wait while the express roared by on the main track. As he was standing outside the train waiting, he heard the shriek of the whistle of the approaching express, roaring down the tracks at tremendous speed and saw the light come into view a great distance away. Then he noticed to his horror that the switch had not been thrown and was still open. The express train would be diverted onto that same side track—and there would be an enormous collision killing hundreds of people if the switch were not closed. With his heart pounding he cried out, "Pull the switch!" And just at the last moment, the switch was thrown and the express roared by down the main track.

I thought: That is the way it is with life. We are waiting a short pause before our destination, but the express train of God's judgment is coming. It may seem like it travels very slowly. But, cosmically speaking, over the ages it has been coming with tremendous speed upon us; and surely there will be a tremendous smashup, and many will be condemned to hell, unless they have "pulled the switch," diverting the judgment they deserve onto Jesus Christ who took it for us on the cross.

That is what it means to be a Christian. That is what it means to be part of the holy catholic church of Jesus Christ. It means that in your soul you have pulled the switch. You have said, "O, God, I accept Him who there, standing in the middle of that track, takes the full brunt of that judgment in my place." Otherwise, surely, that judgment will come right in upon you. Have you made that decision? That verdict? That determination that Christ will be your Savior and your Lord? If so, then you are a part of that church.

As far as many people are concerned, you are the only church that they know. "Let the church be the church" it is declared. As an agent of reconciliation, as a witness for Jesus Christ, this week determine that you are going to be the church, that church which you profess every week to believe in: "I believe in the holy catholic church."

CHAPTER 14

The Communion of the Saints

"That which we have seen and heard declare we unto you, that ye also may have fellowship with us; and truly our fellowship is with the Father, and with his Son, Jesus Christ."

1 John 1:3

THE COMMUNION of the saints is described in the New Testament by the word *koinonia*. This is a Greek word and yet one which is coming more and more to be used in English. In fact, I think that before long it will be, as so many other borrowed words have become, a part of the lingua franca of America. I have read it so many times recently. There are now books on Koinonia; there are societies of Koinonia; there are Koinonia groups and Koinonia materials. I think that soon it will be a word familiar to all Christians. Perhaps by now you have guessed its meaning. Koinonia means, as best we might describe it in English (though this is a very limited definition), *fellowship,* and it comes from the root which means to have a part in, to share in, to participate in.

One of the most distinguishing characteristics of the early church was this vital communion, fellowship or Koinonia which they shared. We read of the early church in Acts, that they continued steadfastly in the Apostles' doctrine and fellowship. I think we need very much in this day to grasp what they meant by this fellowship. If ever a generation needed it ours does. We live in a depersonalized world, an automated world where we must remember our area code, our zip code, our social security number—even our income tax is checked by a computer. In most colleges the students are known by a number; seldom is their name known or is there any concern with their lives. There is a great need for fellowship.

I think perhaps one of the secrets of the success of the Communists is the fact that they have made men comrades. People secretly seek for some sort of camaraderie, some sort of fellowship. But, though Marx could make men and women comrades, only Christ can make us brothers and sisters.

I believe that the church, for the most part, has failed to enter into almost everything that God meant us to; we have claimed little of the land that God has promised to us. Also, we have failed to enter into the depth and meaning of the fellowship that Christ meant for us. So let's look at what is meant by that type of fellowship. It means "a sharing of life." It means that one life is flowing through all of those who live in Jesus Christ. The early church was very much aware that in some secret and mysterious way they had been made one. They were one temple, though living stones; they were one vine, though many branches; they were one family, though many children; there was one life that flowed through each one of their hearts. In this confluence of life they discovered something that made their lives rich and meaningful.

We know that the early church in Jerusalem even went to the extreme of sharing all of their goods, so a communal type of life developed there shortly after Pentecost. They sold all that they had and shared it with one another. Now this is not to be mistaken for communism, though many have taken it as a pretense for advocating that the Bible teaches communism. It is completely different. The Bible teaches private ownership of property. For example, Peter said to Ananias, "While it remained was it not your own? While it remained was it not in your power to do what you would with it?" Communism, on the other hand, teaches that all property belongs to the state.

Secondly, the property was given to the church, not the state. Now if anything is completely foreign to the ideology flowing from Moscow or Peking, it is the idea that everybody ought to give up everything they've got to the church. If that is communism I think Marx would turn over in his grave.

And thirdly, and most importantly of all, the Christians' giving was voluntary. This sets it worlds apart from modern communism which relies above everything else upon the mailed fist of force. Communism doesn't say, "I will give what I have to you." Communism says, "I will take what you have and give it to whomsoever I please."

There was this communal life which was an expression of the one life that existed in each of these: a vital, dynamic life. How pale is the modern reproduction of that Koinonia fellowship! As someone said, "We bounce around our fellowship halls like billiard balls ricocheting off the walls when in truth we ought to be crushed together like grapes." How superficial our fellowship often is.

Let us look and see how John describes this fellowship in his first epistle. He begins by describing some hard cold facts: "That which was from the beginning, which we have heard, which we have seen with our eyes, which we have looked upon, and our hands have handled, of the Word of life. . . . That which we have seen and heard declare we unto you, that ye also may have fellowship with us; and truly our fellowship is with the Father, and with his Son, Jesus Christ" (1John 1:1, 3). The basis of our fellowship, the basis of this Koinonia, is in the living, risen Christ. John was saying, "We are not fools. This is no cunningly devised fable; this is no sentimentality. This is real hard fact. Christ is alive. We saw Him. We touched Him. He is alive and our fellowship is real and will be eternal. It was the Word of life eternal that was manifest unto us."

He begins with the facts. The second point that he brings out is the proclamation of that fact: "That which we have seen and heard, declare we unto you." And so it is ever that if there is going to be true fellowship, it must be based upon a living proclamation, heralding forth the glad tidings of the gospel.

But what was his purpose? (A purpose often missed in our witness is described here when he says, "that you also might have fellowship with us.") People living in a depersonalized world, alienated from their brethren, lonely and without hope in this world and the world to come, might enter into the most blessed fellowship that the world has ever known. I am confident of one thing. Regardless of how anemic is the fellowship that we now have, regardless of how much greater it could be (and by the grace of God is going to be), it is still the greatest fellowship that has ever existed on the face of the earth.

The oneness that Jesus Christ puts into our hearts with those who are fellow believers is something tremendous to know and to experience. I have found that wherever I go in the world, if I meet a person who has received the living, resurrected Christ, that I am his brother and he is mine. This is a thrilling thing. Whether he is a Turk, or an Arab, or a Jew, or a Greek, or a Roman, if he knows the living Christ he is my brother. When this happens to you, within a few minutes you know that there is something in that person that is not in other people. For you share the same light from heaven; the same vitalizing principle dwells in you; you have the same hope; you worship the same Christ. This fellowship is not only with one another, but it is also with the Father and with Jesus Christ. The Bible says we can have no fellowship with God without Christ. The Bible says we cannot know God without Christ. The Bible says we cannot worship God unless we worship Christ. And our fellowship is with Him. This is how we have come to know Him. This is how we have entered into this relationship of Koinonia with God where we share in His life, and Christ shares His life in us. We have this mutual participation. What a blessed fellowship that is. That fellowship, having descended vertically from God, now is to move horizontally among the brethren.

Then John continues with this very important verse: "These things write we unto you, that your joy may be full" (v. 4).

I missed the context of that verse for years. Many times I read, "We write these things that your joy may be full." But what are "these things"? That you may know Christ; that you may trust Him; that you may know His love and His life. But that is not all that John said. It is just part of it. "That you might have fellowship with him," yes, but, "with us also, that your joy may be full." Those who live a solitary Christian life do not know the fullness of joy that God meant them to know. Those who have never come to the place of really sharing their lives with others and entering into a spiritual fellowship have never known the fullness of joy.

Would you have joy in your life? Then cultivate, seek after, and pursue a fellowship of love and sharing, a deep commitment of life one to another. You should have a Christian friend. Even Christian in *Pilgrim's Progress* had "Faithful." David had his Jonathan; Luther had his Melanchthon; Calvin his Beza. They shared their lives together and thus the fullness of the life of Christ, which is meant to be lived in a corporate situation, was known.

Do you have a real Christian friend? A friend with whom you share Christ? Do you want to see a deepening of that fellowship? Then I say to you, "Get down on your knees with that person and share the things of God together." How long has it been since you were with some friend on your knees together in prayer . . . confessing your faults . . . praying for one another . . . helping one another on the way which leads to life eternal . . . strengthening one another . . . sharing mutual burdens and woes? If you do this you will begin to know something of a fellowship that you may not have known before, "that your joy may be full."

But John continues to describe an essential prerequisite for this fellowship. The Bible says that in God there is no darkness, for God is light and if we walk in *that light* then we have fellowship with one another. That is *light* which reveals, which makes transparent, which makes luminous and clear and plain and readable. Are you walking in the light or are you walking in darkness, covering your life with a veil, hiding your secret sins from God and others? Are you letting people know what you are, or what you are not?

What a wonderful thing it is when you determine that you are really going to seek after God, that you are going to walk in the light. The Bible teaches us to confess our faults one to another, and to pray for one another. How little of this is done today. Consequently people live behind a crusty veneer. They live lonely lives in the midst of crowds. They are unhappy, without any real friend with whom they can share their lives. There is always a pretense. There is always hypocrisy, a hiding behind the mask. They never really get out into the light and let their life flow through to another.

The Scripture also says, "The blood of Jesus Christ, his Son, cleanseth us from all sin." How true this is. When we really get honest with one another we find that our sanctification progresses, and we are cleansed from our sin, not only from its guilt but also from its power. And to those who would pretend that they have no sin, John says, "they deceive themselves and the truth is not in them."

One of the great movements in America today is the movement toward fellowship groups—small Koinonia groups which are springing up all over the land, where people participate in and share with one another in a confluence of heart and life. Four, six, eight or ten people together, reading the Bible, praying, sharing testimonies of their strength and victories, asking one another to pray for them, finding their lives utterly transformed, encouraging one another and finding strength that they had never known before.

The Bible says in Hebrews that we are to be careful to provoke one another to good works. I would encourage you that if you don't have someone, or some group, that you call a group of Christians together with you and get serious with God. Get honest with God and with one another. Share the life that Christ has given to you and you will find in the blessed experience of true Koinonia the fullness of the joy that Christ meant for you to have. Christ shared His life. He poured out His life, His blood for us. May we share that life one with another, and heal wounded, lonely hearts. Bring the stranger into the fellowship which truly is with the Father and with His Son, Jesus Christ.

CHAPTER 15

The Forgiveness of Sins

"If we confess our sins, he is faithful and just to forgive us our sins, and to cleanse us from all unrighteousness."

1 John 1:9

NOT FAR from the city of New York is a small cemetery wherein may be found a most unusual grave and headstone. On that headstone there is no name, no date of birth or of death, no epitaph, no fulsome eulogy. There is no embellishment of the sculptor's art. There is, in fact, but one single, solitary word; one all encompassing word of three short syllables: FORGIVEN.

Mankind's Greatest Need: Forgiveness

But that is the most important word that can be recorded about any human being who has ever walked upon earth since it is true that the trail of the serpent has left its slime upon every human soul. And since it is true that sin is endemic to the human race—from the pauper in his cottage to the king on his throne—and since it is true that the judge of all the earth has pronounced His verdict of "guilty as charged" and not one of us can endure the execution of that condemnation, forgiveness is the universally greatest need of all mankind. Here is an illustration of that need:

A man was several hundred miles beyond civilization, in the far northern reaches of Canada. What misfortunes had befallen him we are not told. But his journey had, at long last, come to its end. He was seated in a small hut which he had constructed. His food had long since run out. An inverted pie pan

on his knees served as a writing desk and in his skeleton hand
was a letter which he had been writing to his mother when
death overtook him. In that letter the man said that it had been
more than forty days since he had seen a human being, that his
food had long ago run out, and that it seemed that there was no
more blood left in him because it had been so long since he had
eaten. He said that he could only walk a few steps now and,
surely, soon the end must come. Only one thought, one all-en-
compassing thought filled his mind night and day: Would God
forgive his sins? And every sentient creature who has lived his
life beneath the gaze of the Almighty must surely ask himself
that same question: Will God forgive my sins?

I am happy that we have come in our study of the Apostles'
Creed to the great pinnacle of its declarations: "I believe in the
forgiveness of sins." As the Psalmist declared; "There is forgiveness with thee, that thou mayest be feared" (Psalms 130:4).
Yes, the great glory of the Christian faith is its affirmation of
the forgiveness of sins.

Some people, however, do not believe that such a thing is
even needed. A recent survey in France indicated that 90 percent of the people there do not believe that there is such a thing
as personal sin. The Marxist, in answer to the question, "Is
there such a thing as sin?" would aver that there is not. He
would try to prove it is simply an economic problem—and
when more money is provided for the poor, then sin, so called,
will disappear. And yet he ignores the obvious sins of the rich
and the blatant sins, the heinous sins, which still exist in the
Soviet Union and in China.

The behaviorist says, "No, there is no such thing as sin; all is
simply stimulus and response. Man is not responsible for what
he does. Sin is an anachronism long forgotten by the educated." The evolutionist will tell you that there is no such thing
as sin, and that man has not fallen into sin. If there was any fall
at all, man fell up the stairs on his progess from the tiger and
the ape to a human being. And whatever residue remains of
that which men call sin will also disappear with progress.

But in contradistinction to all of these, the Bible very clearly declares that "all have sinned, and come short of the glory of God" (Romans 3:23). Christ declared that it was for our sins that He died, and God tells us that "there is none righteous, no not one" (Romans 3:10). I believe, further, that the conscience of every honest person must admit to those sentiments that say: "I have sinned before Thee and am not worthy to be called Thy child" (*see* Luke 15:18, 19).

What is sin? Having asked a lot of people that question, the one thing I have noticed is that today the average American really doesn't have the foggiest idea of what sin is. For some people, sin is simply what other people do. For yet another group, sin is like that character in Alice in Wonderland who was asked what his words meant, and he said that his words meant whatever he meant for them to mean; that is, they meant nothing at all except what he wanted them to be. And some people are quite determined that sin will be whatever they say it is. If they want to commit a particular sin, then by definition that is ruled out as a sin.

But the Scripture is clear that sin is any want of conformity to or transgression of the Law of God. Sin is something which every human being, deep in his heart, knows that he has committed against the holy God of heaven.

Is there forgiveness for sin? Some people do not like the very idea of forgiveness. They are the lineal descendants of the Pharisees. Their number is legion. They are like the elder brother in the Parable of the Prodigal Son, who was angry when he heard that the son who had wasted his inheritance in riotous living had returned to the homestead and had been forgiven by the father. He was as angry as that person who said to me one time, "Do you mean to tell me that a person can live for seventy years a wicked and godless and sinful life and then be forgiven?" The very idea was reprehensible to him.

But then there is the thief on the cross, guilty of capital crimes and receiving the due reward for his deeds. He received the gracious forgiveness of Christ: "Today shalt thou be with me in paradise" (Luke 23:43). The glory of the Christian religion is the glory of its grace that we may be forgiven by the grace of God, regardless of what we have done.

"Isn't that too easy?" say some. Well, it is easy to receive a gift. It is easy for us to receive the forgiveness of Christ, but it was not easy for Christ to procure it.

What Is Forgiveness?

Paul says that "in [Him] we have redemption through his blood, the forgiveness of sins, according to the riches of his grace" (Ephesians 1:7). What is forgiveness of sins? This text says that it is redemption through the blood of Jesus Christ. Jesus was like the high priest in the Old Testament who, on the Day of Atonement, entered into the Holy of Holies, into that most holy place beyond the veil of blue and scarlet and crimson. Even then the high priest could not enter in without first having slain the bullock to bring blood to offer for his own sins and to make the confession, "I, O Jehovah, I and my house have committed iniquity and have transgressed against Thy holy law."

And having entered in with the hot coals and the incense, he would drop the incense under the coals to fill the holiest place with the fragrance of the incense—to blot out the stench of his sin. Then he would sprinkle the blood upon the mercy seat so that he could return with the blood of the sacrifice for the sins of the whole people of Israel. Only thus could forgiveness be obtained.

All of that was but a great picture of Jesus Christ, the great high priest, who would enter in beyond the veil of death, into the outer darkness where dwelt the Shekinah glory of God. Into the pit of that death went Christ without blood, without the blood of lambs or bulls or goats, and without even the confession of sin. "Which of you," He said, "convinceth me of sin" (John 8:46).

But Jesus entered in with His own blood: Bearing our sin, He entered into that place. God looked down upon His own

Son, now bearing the guilt of the world, and unsheathed the glittering sword of His own recompense and smote His own Son. There He bent the mighty bow of His justice and loosed the arrows of His retribution into the very soul of Christ.

As the prophet said, "He hath bent his bow, and set me as a mark for the arrow. He hath caused the arrows of his quiver to enter into my reins" (Lamentations 3:12, 13). So Christ endured in body and soul the penalty for our sins. Then, on that glorious Easter morning, the great high priest ushered forth again into the light of day, and sent the hearts of men and women ringing throughout the world. He, who is our eternal song, has placed a song in the hearts of all of those who believe. We have, in Him, redemption through His blood. This is the forgiveness of sins. Forgiveness may not be obtained anywhere else but in Jesus Christ.

I am amazed at how many people suppose that apart from Christ and trusting in Him, they can find forgiveness. I remember a woman who told me once that she had prayed every day of her life for sixty-five years to be forgiven and that she had never been forgiven for one sin—until that day that she accepted Christ as her Savior. Then she knew in her heart that the burden was lifted, that her guilt was gone, and that her sins were forgiven. She had come to experience the forgiveness of sins.

Forgiveness by His Grace

We have the forgiveness of sins, said Paul, "according to the riches of his grace." That is the measure of the forgiveness that we have—according to the riches of His grace. And how vast are those riches! We have so many other measuring sticks for our forgiveness. We suppose that we have forgiveness according to the smallness of our sins. If we just don't do anything really bad, then perhaps we will obtain forgiveness. But that is not the way it works at all. Even in human relationships, you and I know that it is not the size of the offense—it is the size of the soul of the person against whom you offend. There are some people who are so broad-souled and magnanimous that the greatest offense will be forgiven. There are others who are so narrow-souled and mean-spirited that the least word will cause offense, an offense that will be savored and remembered and dredged up out of the slime of memory years later to be waggled in your face. No. It is not the size of your sin; it is the size of the soul of the one against whom you sin. And our God is a God of all grace, a God of infinite mercy and forgiveness.

Some people suppose that it's the length of the time that they sin: "Oh, if only I had not continued so long in my wicked ways. But now I am old and my soul is set as concrete. The wrinkles are on my brow; my sin is ineffaceable; there is no hope yet for me." Ah, my friend, it matters not whether you are a babe or a Methuselah, if you come to Jesus Christ the blood of Christ cleanses us from all sin.

It is not a matter of the size of our sorrow, the depth of our contrition. No. It is a matter of the riches of His grace. Paul tells us that it is not even a matter of the strength of our faith. God says that He will not break the bruised reed or quench the smoking flax. If our faith is as weak as a reed which has been bruised, or as feeble as the flax which has nothing left but smoke, that will not be broken nor quenched. It is according to the riches of His grace—the inestimable, unsearchable, ineffable riches of the grace of God that we have forgiveness.

The Requirements for Grace

But God has laid down very clearly what are the requirements to receive that illimitable forgiveness.

We must, first of all, recognize our sins. So many people want to simply maintain their goodness and profess their morality. They want to claim that they are innocent. But the first requirement is that they change their plea from innocent to guity-as-charged and acknowledge their sin. It has always been true that those who have been the closest to God have known themselves to be in the deepest of sin.

Job's patience is legend, but compared to him each of us

would seem to be an irascible and impatient child. Job, when he saw God in His glory, said: "I have heard of thee by the hearing of the ear but now mine eye seeth thee. Wherefore I abhor myself, and repent in dust and ashes" (Job 42:5, 6). Or that seraphic prophet Isaiah, who, when he saw the Lord high and lifted up, said, "I am a man of unclean lips, and I dwell in the midst of a people of unclean lips . . ." (Isaiah 6:5). Or the great Apostle Peter, who said, "Lord, depart from me for I am a sinful man" (see Luke 5:8). Or the Apostle Paul, who said, "I am the chief of sinners" (see 1 Timothy 1:15). Or Augustine, whose name is not mentioned without the prefix "Saint," who is famous for his book, *The Confessions of Saint Augustine.*

No. Those who have drawn closest to the light which is God have seen the depths of the stains of the serpent upon their souls. And those who suppose themselves to be "quite all right, thank you," are simply giving evidence that they dwell in darkness far away in a land far removed from the light and grace of God.

We must recognize our sin. We must confess our sin. We must be willing to acknowledge it before God and we must be willing to repent of it.

"What is repentance?" asked the preacher to the catechism class of young girls. One of them said, "That is to be sorry for our sins."

"How sorry?" asked the preacher. And the second replied, "To be sorry enough to cry."

And he asked another who said, "To be sorry enough to quit." Out of the mouths of babes we have a pretty good definition of what repentance really is. But beyond that there must be faith in Jesus Christ without whom there is no hope of forgiveness at all. It is only in Christ that we have that forgiveness, as we reach out our hand and place our trust in Him.

In the Old Testament, the priest would lay his hands upon the sacrificial lamb, confess the sins of the people, and then draw his hands away. That mysterious imputation took place so that the guilt of the people would be laid upon the head of the lamb that was taken away and slain. What is it to have faith in Christ? It is, as Isaac Watts said:

> My faith would lay her hand
> On that dear head of Thine,
> While like a penitent I stand
> And thus confess my sins.

Could you imagine yourself today with your hands upon the head of Christ, confessing your sins, acknowledging your guilt, enumerating your transgressions and then drawing them away—knowing that God the Father has imputed unto His own beloved Son all of your guilt and sin? And now Jesus Christ goes off into a land uninhabited, into the darkness of death, to descend into the pit where there is no light of stars, or sun to relieve the blackness of that isolation. There He endures in body and soul the infinite wrath of God in your place. *That* is the price of the forgiveness of your sins. And that is what it means to trust in Jesus Christ. "In [Him] we have redemption through his blood, the forgiveness of sins, according to the riches of his grace."

Can you know that you have been forgiven? My friends, there is nothing in this world more important than your knowing that you have been forgiven.

Someone once asked Martin Luther: "Doctor Luther, do you feel that you have been forgiven?" "No," he replied, "but I am as sure as I am that there is a God in heaven."

> For feelings come, and feelings go,
> And feelings are deceiving.
> My warrant is the Word of God,
> Naught else is worth believing.

Have you felt the heavy hand of guilt upon your shoulder, pressing you down and threatening to squeeze out your very life? Have you felt the suffocating presence of your sin as it tends to blot out all your light and joy? If you have ever felt that way, then there is good news for you: There is forgiveness by God! That forgiveness is to be found in faith in Jesus Christ. And I would urge you, right now, to reach out that hand of faith and place it upon the head of the Lamb of God, who takes away the sins of the world. May it be that, whether literally or figuratively, when someone visits your grave he may find there written upon your headstone the word: FORGIVEN.

CHAPTER 16

The Resurrection of the Body

> *"In a moment, in the twinkling of an eye, at the last trump: for the trumpet shall sound, and the dead shall be raised incorruptible, and we shall be changed."*
>
> *1 Corinthians 15:52*

IT IS an exciting and unforgettable thing to see an army routed and flying in tumultuous retreat. Who can forget the vivid scenes of Napoleon as he retreated from Moscow and dotted the snows of Russia with ninety thousand of the imperial army of France? Or the armies of Hitler as they retreated across France and back through Germany to Berlin? Or the five kings of the Old Testament who fled across rock and hill as they were pursued by Joshua? Indeed, it is an unforgettable thing!

But the text—"death is swallowed up in victory"—announces an even worse discomfiture of another army. For it seems that a grim and ghastly giant proposed to conquer the earth. He was, indeed, the conqueror of all conquerors. Beside him Alexander, Caesar, Hannibal, and Napoleon all paled by comparison. In fact, each of them met him and was himself defeated. His name is Death!

He carried a black flag and took no prisoners. He dug a trench across the hemispheres and contemptuously filled it with the carcasses of the nations. He gathered together his hosts, an army of all the aches and pains and maladies and infirmities which have ever plagued the human race. It was, indeed, an awesome force to behold. There were legions of leprosy and columns of cancer, squadrons of sicknesses of every sort, and phalanxes of infection. There were cohorts of consumption and armies of apoplexy, horsemen of heart attacks, and platoons of pestilence. There were the fusiliers of feculence and dragoons of decay. It was, indeed, the most fearful, the most formidable army which had ever been arrayed.

He drilled them in the cold northeast wind and amidst the slush of the melting snow. He pitched the tents of the charnel house. Indeed, he threw up the embankments of the cemetery mount. Most he slew with a single blow of his axe; others were taken by long sieges of evil habits. He knocked with his bony hand at the doors of hospitals and sick rooms, and none could withstand his advance: Presidents and kings, sultans and czars fell alike beneath the wheels of his war chariot. He was the victor in all battles.

None could stay his hand or stop his advance, until . . . until that day when there appeared in the east one whose countenance was like the morning, one who strode forward unafraid and indeed entered into the very lair of this giant himself. Spurgeon has said that He scattered the night of death like the rising sun. He gave no bone to Cerberus, that ferocious dog of the giant, Death, but rather cut off his head and grasped hold of the beast and cast it away.

Like Samson in Gaza, He tore up the gates of death and carried away the bars of the grave. Like David, He delivered His flock out of the jaws of the lion and grasped the beast by his mane and slew him. Like Abraham, He returned triumphantly from the slaughter of the kings. Like Moses, He delivered Israel out of the house of bondage.

He came as a great king and captain, and in that well-fought fight He emerged victorious. Coming forth from that darksome battle in the grave, He held in His left hand the torn-off bolt of the sepulcher, and in His right hand the key to all the cemeteries of the world.

And now, soon, He comes with ten thousand times ten thousand of His saints, with an outstretched arm and a high hand—and He drags behind Him that defeated foe, the grim prince of the realm of nightshade. Death has been conquered! Indeed, that old braggart, Death, has lost his crown; he has lost his scepter; he has lost his palace; he has even lost his fearlessness. "Death, where is thy victory. . . . where is thy sting?"

Indeed, over every mausoleum, every catacomb, every necropolis, on every cenotaph—indeed, on every sarcophagus—there must be written one word, the single word—Victory. Christ has won the victory. Death is swallowed up in victory. Thank God for the victory of the resurrection! "I believe in the resurrection of the dead." And that resurrection which was accomplished by Christ is the seal and the pledge of ours.

The Nature of Our Resurrection

It is interesting, I think, to note that in every passage that describes that great "wakin' up morning" which is to come, that great resurrection day when we shall be joined together with our Savior, we always see that it is accompanied by great sounds. There is, indeed, the voice of the archangel, the shout of God, the trump of God, and that sound has a very penetrating effect. It penetrates all the way into the silence of the mausoleum, undisturbed for a thousand years. It penetrates all the way into the depths of the sea, to the coral caves where thousands have lain for centuries. It penetrates into the silence of cemeteries and into ancient crypts—a silence that will be shattered by that sound of a trumpet when Christ shall come.

When Christ shall come on that great resurrection day, in one terrific shudder the graves will heave up like the waves of the sea, and the once-dead will stalk forth on the lurid air. For Christ is the first fruits and we, which are Christ's, will be there at His coming.

Do you remember the Hebrew festivals? First of all, there was the Passover, during which time the paschal lamb was slain. The next day was a sabbath day, a day of rest. Then came the first day of the week, when the first fruits of the harvest were brought into the temple. Then the wave offering was presented as those fruits were waved back and forth signifying the sanctifying of the rest of the harvest.

And so it is with Christ, the first fruits from among the dead. First came the Passover when Christ, our paschal lamb, was slain for us. Then following the sabbath day, when He rested in the realm of death, the first day of the week arrived, the day of the feast of the first fruits when Christ was offered up to God and appeared alive again. And going back and forth, to and fro, like a wave offering among His people, He sanctified the whole harvest which is yet to come.

A Bodily Resurrection

The resurrection of the dead! What a glorious truth that is! And Christ has shown, by His resurrection, that there is in the ultimate constitution of this universe a higher law than death. We see that death is for life, and not life for death. Jesus Christ actually rose again from the dead, says Paul. He appeared to Cephas, to the twelve, and to over five hundred brethren at once. Then to James and, finally, to Paul. By incontrovertible evidence, He showed Himself alive and also made a pledge that because He lives, we who trust in Him will live also.

How important is this doctrine of the resurrection! You know that it is unique with Christianity. All of the pagan religions believe in the immortality of the soul. But beyond that, only Christianity teaches the resurrection of the body. Plato declared that the soul would survive the body, but he, like the rest of the Greeks, knew nothing of the resurrection of the body. We have no vague and shadowy hope of some strange existence like Casper, the Ghost. What we do have is a solid and substantial hope that our bodies shall be raised once more.

Tertullian, in the second century, emphasized the importance of the resurrection when he said: "He, therefore, will not be a Christian who shall deny this doctrine which is confessed by Christians—the doctrine which is alien to paganism. The resurrection of the dead is the Christian's hope."

But what is the nature of this resurrection of the body? "With what body do they come?" asked Paul rhetorically. Two errors have accompanied that question: Some have said that we come forth with exactly the same molecules that were put into the grave; others have said, on the contrary, that we are entirely a new creation. Somewhere between this Scylla and Charybdis I think there is a deep tide of water through which we might sail to understand what the Bible says. The idea that exactly the same molecules will come forth to recreate or re-form the same body is not a concept supported by Scripture. The skeptics have raised questions about a person who loses a leg in China and an arm in England and is buried in America. Are we, in that last day, going to have human body parts flying through the air? The whole doctrine is brought into disrepute.

And what about old Roger Williams, the founder of the Baptist church in Rhode Island and governor of that state? When they dug up his casket to move him, they discovered that the root of an apple tree had opened the casket lid and had gone in and had sucked poor Roger right out of the box. The tree had used his molecules for the making of bright red apples which had been eaten by who knows how many people. Now, where do we get the molecules to rebuild old Roger Williams?

"Thou foolish one," said Paul, "that which thou sowest is not that which will come up again" (see 1 Corinthians 15:36). We place a tiny seed in the ground and a beautiful rose or a lily comes forth—but the seed dies. Likewise, we plant an acorn and an oak tree comes out. No! We do not sow the body that shall be. It is the same and yet it is different. As we have heard sung so beautifully: "We shall be changed."

And what a transformation that will be! We shall have a new body, a spiritual body. But do not suppose that that spiritual body will be a body which is immaterial. That is not what the word means. There are spiritual people today who are not immaterial ghosts, and there are also those who are carnal. This refers to that which their hearts are given to and that which they are adapted toward. We shall have a body adapted to spiritual ends, but we shall also have material bodies—bodies that will be changed.

Body Will Be Joined to Soul

One man visited the home of a friend and discovered to his surprise that the front and back yards were filled with debris— the debris of carpenters and all sorts of workmen. When he made his way through that debris, he noticed that not a room in the house had been left alone. There was not a room in which a person could live. All of the pictures were off the walls and the paperhangers and the painters were at work. The roof was being torn up to put in cupolas, and rooms were being added onto the back. The entire kitchen was being changed and refurbished with new equipment and facilities. The whole house was being transformed.

He discovered upon inquiring that the inhabitants of that home had gone on a six-month trip to the Holy Land. What a joyful thing that must have been for this family to see the entirely transformed and enlarged home with all of the new and wonderful facilities! And so it is with us in our bodies. There will come a time when our souls will make that trip to the land which is holy, but our bodies will be torn apart by the ravages of time and cold and heat. They will not be fit to live in: But there will come a day when the archangelic reveille will sound, and then our body will be reconstructed in a glorious and transformed manner and rejoined with our souls.

Our bodies and souls are friends of long standing. They do sympathize, one with the other. And what a day of joy that will be when they are joined once more together! They will be the same and yet they will be different. How will they be different?

Our Glorious Body

For one thing, they will be glorious bodies, like Christ's glorious body.

In the summer of 1983, in the Louvre in Paris, I saw the

statue of Venus, that magnificent piece of sculpture. One can go right up to that statue and even touch it. I noticed, when I drew close to it, the tremendous ravages of time. It is pitted and pockmarked all over and is filled with all sorts of blotches and cracks. Time has done its worst. Similarly, time has done its worst to us. Through the ages of mutations and through the years of our life, time has done its best to destroy us. And I am sure that the bodies that we have then will be as different as the body of an Olympic gold-medal winner is different from the body of the most emaciated wretch in a hospital or lazaretto. Indeed, we shall have a glorious body.

A Perfect Body

Secondly, ours will be perfect bodies. Will a child be raised up as an infant, as an old man? Of course not! An acorn is not raised as an acorn but as an oak tree. In the fullness of manhood or womanhood we will be raised. And all of our imperfections will be done away with.

Will we be fat or skinny? No! I think we will be perfect. I recently saw on television a new operation where they stick some sort of a suction tube in a person's stomach or legs and pull out all the fat. And the obese are made trim. I thought how clumsy will be that operation when compared to the operation that God is going to perform on some of us. Indeed, in that day, there will be no obesity. I am sure there will be no rotunds under the rotunda of heaven.

The early church father, Origen, said that, among all the geometric shapes, the sphere was the most perfect of shapes; and therefore he thought that we would be spheroid in heaven, since that would be the perfect shape. I have often thought that some Christians are approaching perfection in this realm. But, seriously, I question Origen's understanding of perfect shapes. That may be all right for geometry, but it does not work very well for people. We will be, I am sure, beautiful and handsome persons. Everyone has lurking within him a perfect human being. Of all different types, whoever you are, whatever you are, there is a perfect you that is just dying to get out. It will take a little work in some cases, a little more in others. But I am sure that, when God is finished, we will be what God eternally means for us to be.

An Immortal Body

Furthermore, we will have immortal bodies—bodies which will know no sickness or decay. We are born adying in this world. Sicknesses clamor to pull us down beneath the turf. But in that day, there will be no more coughs or aches; there will be no more arthritis or rheumatism; there will be no flutter of heart or shortness of breath; there will be no spectacles or hearing aids or false teeth. Indeed, there will be no supports for the arches. We will need no such things as that. We will be changed. We will be new.

An Untiring Body

Fourthly, we will also be untiring, for the Scripture says that we will not sleep. There is no night there. We will never weary nor grow tired. Some of us, after a long day, can barely drag ourselves to bed at night. Some have reached the stage where the best part of the day ends when the alarm clock goes off in the morning. They can hardly drag themselves out of bed each morning. There is so much to do and so little strength with which to do it. We find ourselves, it seems, gathering and collecting and hoarding that strength more and more as the years go by, wondering why God wastes all that energy on children.

But in that day we will be without fatigue; we will never grow tired; we will do anything that we want. And when we get finished we will be as energetic as when we started! Whatever our desires are, whatever our inclinations, whatever talents that God has given us, we will continue with those things to perfection. What a glorious thing that will be! What a magnificent body God will provide in that resurrection day when we will be changed. Indeed, as I contemplate those changes, gladly could I fling aside this old body, filled with aches and pains, and look forward to that new and resurrected body which Christ has prepared.

Will we recognize one another in heaven? Well, I am sure that we will. They recognized Moses and Elijah on the Mount of Transfiguration and I am sure that since love is eternal that God would not have us enter into paradise without knowing those whom we have loved and lost.

Who is it that will be resurrected? Is it only the redeemed? No. The Scripture says that all that are in the graves shall come forth, some to the resurrection of life and others to the resurrection of damnation. Yes, indeed, there are some that will come forth who might wish that they could stay in a hole in the ground. Their bodies, I am sure, will be the embodiment of the evil passions which have consumed them and have wrought so heinously within them during their lives. And they will go forth to that punishment which, while in the body, they brought upon themselves as they so gladly cooperated in the sins which are the cause thereof.

Where Do We Go at Death?

But what happens in the intermediate state, between now and the resurrection? At death, our souls go immediately to be with the Lord if we belong to Him, and souls of the wicked are cast immediately into hell. The body remains in the ground awaiting that great resurrection morning when Christ will call us forth to be joined together again with our souls. The souls of the wicked are cast into condemnation and the souls of the righteous are "with the Lord." Besides these two places, the Scripture acknowledges no other place for the soul separated from the body.

Yes, a resurrection day is coming. It will be a glorious day for some and a horrid one for others. I hope that you know that glorious hope, the hope that is ours only through Jesus Christ. You can have that assurance if only you will trust in Jesus Christ. And then, for you, Death, the king of terrors that has held the whole world in bondage through fear all these centuries, will have lost his grip: you will not fear his terror. Indeed, you can say, "O death, where is thy sting? O grave, where is thy victory? . . . thanks be to God, which giveth us the victory through our Lord Jesus Christ" (1 Corinthians 15:55, 57). Death is swallowed up in victory. Yes, I believe in the resurrection of the dead.

CHAPTER 17

The Life Everlasting

*"And God shall wipe away all tears from their eyes;
and there shall be no more death, neither sorrow,
nor crying, neither shall there be any more pain: for
the former things are passed away."*

Revelation 21:4

WE COME at last to the final affirmation of the Apostles' Creed:
"I believe in the life everlasting." This is the great climacteric
of the Creed—the final conclusion of all things in our faith—
the life everlasting. Without this, then, all of the rest of the
Creed would be meaningless and in vain. Indeed, what would
it suffice to say that I believe in God, the Creator, if there were
no life eternal? Then He would have simply made us that we
should rot and corrupt in the grave. What would it mean to say
that we believe in Jesus Christ, the divine Redeemer, who died
and rose again, if we shall die and never rise again? What
would it do to say that we believe in the Holy Spirit if we do
not believe that that Spirit will raise our mortal bodies?

No. Without the belief in the life everlasting, all of the Creed
is devoid of meaning. In fact, without a belief in everlasting
life, all of *life* is devoid of meaning. And that is one of the great
tragedies of our modern secular society.

The word *secular* comes from the Latin term which means
"time." It is a particular type of word for time, however, in
Latin, because it is that word which describes time as it is conceived in this life only, without regard to any life beyond. It is a
concept of life that is bounded by the grave, a view of life that
looks not beyond the mortician's bench. It sees no hope be-

yond the dark horizon of the tomb. And it is with that tragic view of life that secularism is seeping into the souls of modern men and is depriving their lives of meaning and significance and value. That is why, in an eight-year period, some 39,000 young people between fifteen and twenty-four have committed suicide in America.

Recently I wrote letters to the Senate and the House, urging them to pass an anti-suicide bill that was before committee. But I am sure that as long as our educational system is thoroughly enmeshed in secularism and as long as God is banished from our classrooms, this phenomenon of teen-age suicides is going to continue regardless of what is done. Tragic, indeed, that such a narrowing of the view of life could come now when all other views are expanding so magnificently. Everlasting life! No term boggles the mind as does that one!

When I was a child I did what I would assume every other young person does. Did you not reach some state in your life when you wrestled with the terms of *everlasting, eternity, forever, endlessness*? What do they mean? I said to myself that the universe is eternal. Where would you end up if you went straight out and out and out. You must, at last, finally come to something, I thought.

Ah, I thought, *at last you will come to a wall. And what,* said my mind, *is on the other side of the wall? Oh,* I said, *it is a very thick wall. But surely, at last, we must finally come to the other side of the wall. And what then?* Well, at that time, with wearied brain, I would usually turn over and go to sleep!

If infinity in space cannot be measured, how much more is it impossible for us to measure eternity in time? When shall forever be over? Well, let me tell you so that you will know. Imagine, if you can, that the strongest angel that God has ever created would stretch forth his mighty pinions and raise himself up from this planet and set forth out into space—on beyond the colossus of Jupiter and the rings of Saturn, out past Uranus and Neptune to that planet Pluto that dwells in arctic night. And from there, on beyond the solar system to the farthest star in this galaxy, he goes, and then out into the intergalactic void beyond the Andromeda nebula and past all of the vast billions of galaxies—until at last he comes to the very rim of the universe. There, finding the ecliptic of the universe, he makes the transit around the perimeter of the cosmos and does it over and over again, a million, a billion, a trillion times until finally, totally exhausted, he comes at last to earth once more and folds his wings. Then eternity will have had it—which is never. Never, never!

There is a quaint fable that tells of a great and mighty mountain far, far up in the north. it is a hundred miles long and a hundred miles wide at the base and extends up into the sky a hundred miles in height. It is made of solid and impenetrable granite. Once every thousand years, a little bird flies to the peak of that mountain and sharpens its beak. It then flies away—not to return for a thousand years. And only when that great mountain shall have been totally worn away will one day of eternity have passed.

It is an interesting fable, but, of course, quite untrue because we know that even when ten billion such mountains as that have been totally wiped away, even one second of eternity would not have passed. Forever is a very long time!

What Eternity Will Be Like

For those who belong to Christ, who are the redeemed of God, ". . . eye hath not seen, nor ear heard, neither have entered into the heart of man the things which God hath prepared for them that love him" (1 Corinthians 2:9). If you were to skim the brightest sparkles from the summer seas they would not begin to tell you of the scintillation of the crystal sea of God. If you were to pile up the glories of the most magnificent cities on this earth, one on top of the other, you would not have the haziest notion of the spectacular glory of the city of God.

Can you imagine a place where every house is a mansion or palace, every step is a triumph, every feast is a banquet, every covering of the head is a coronation, every year is a jubilee, every month is an enchantment, every week is a transport of delight, every hour is a paradise, and every moment is an ecstasy? This is the heaven of God! Who can imagine it and who can understand what God has prepared?

Consider the place: There are the new heavens and the new earth where sin shall be no more, where the curse is removed, where entropy ceases. Entropy is the scientific name for the curse of God, where all things decay and disintegrate and go into nothing. The day will come when the great angel of God will reach down a mighty hand and take hold of the wheel of time and proclaim, "Time shall be no more!" And in that moment the curse shall be lifted and entropy shall be gone. For, you see, entropy is simply a measure of time. If you were to have seen me thirty years ago and then look at me today, you would know that time had passed because of the effects of entropy. Every measure of time is simply a measure of entropy. And when time shall be no more, then the curse shall be gone from the world.

From the new heavens to the new earth (for that will be the abode of the righteous, as the greatest of theologians have always maintained)—upon the reconstituted and paradisical earth—a whole new universe will be the home of those who have been redeemed. Then there will be the Holy City, New Jerusalem, descending from heaven as a bride adorned for her husband. What a glorious city that is!

The City of God

What is it like? We are all familiar with the fact that the Scripture says that the city of God, the New Jerusalem, has streets of gold. I remember reading one time the story of one who had experienced clinical death. He found himself speeding rapidly through a long dark tunnel toward a light, and then, bursting out into the air, saw laid out beneath him the New Jerusalem. And he said that he was amazed, as he looked at the towers and the spires and the palaces and the mansions, that the entire city was made of pure gold.

I thought to myself, "Well, now, that is not true. Doesn't that person know anything. Doesn't he know that it is the streets that are made of gold?" I purposely examined the Scripture and found that the city *is* made of pure gold—gold as clear as glass, like crystal. Towers of crystal gold, he saw, and spires made of pure and transparent gold reaching up into the crystalline sky. What a magnificent city that will be. We cannot even imagine the glory of it. What architectural marvels will be there. Can you imagine that the God who fashioned this entire universe would be outdone by someone like Frank Lloyd Wright? What amazing examples of architecture will be seen in that marvelous city of God.

The walls of the city, we are told in Revelation, are made of jasper, a deep, rich green, a transparent color, a magnificent hue. And the twelve gates are each made of a single pearl. Magnificent beyond description. There is no dirt or dust or refuse in that city whose streets are of translucent gold. There is no dirt in those halls of alabaster. That city of ivory and gold is beyond my ability to describe!

Also, there will be magnificent parks there, for we are told that it is a paradise. And paradise comes from the Persian word *paradiso,* which means an enclosed garden or park. We shall have returned to that Edenic bliss! And in that park there will be no fear of muggers and no darkness because there will be no night there; "the Lamb [will be] the light thereof" (Revelation 21:23).

Ah, the glories of that place have never entered into the heart or mind of man. But I hope that some dim explanation of what God has told us may, indeed, ravish our hearts with a desire to go to this place which is far better than any we have known here before.

The People in the City of God

What will the people of that city be like? Well, we know that they will have reached perfection. They will be just men made perfect, justified here and perfected there. They will be perfect in body, with bodies that will never age or grow sick, that will never weary or grow weak, and never need sleep.

And the mind will be put to full use. (We are told that the greatest genius uses not 10 percent of the capacity of his brain.)

We will be totally free to use our minds to the greatest extent, to learn more than we have dreamed about knowing here. Then we shall know even as we are known.

We will have all eternity to examine the great mysteries of the universe which God has created. And the wonders of those mysteries are beyond even our conception. All human inventions and creations may be examined now by those who have the mind for it. But we have never reached the end of any of the creations of God. The deeper we peer into the cell the more complex it grows. We have studied the atom and its electrons, and more and more mysterious things are discovered with every passing year. The farther out we peer into the universe with our greatest telescopes, the more wonders appear—things that only a decade ago would not have been dreamed of. So we will have all eternity to examine the mysteries of God, with new capacities of vision. Now, compared to many birds, which have the most telescopic and microscopic vision, we are almost blind at best. We talk about 20-20 vision. Why, I am sure that when we get to heaven we will look upon that as almost being legally blind.

In that day we will see colors that have never been seen before. Those who have gone on beyond this world and have seen some vision, some presentiment of that which is to come, have said that even the grass is multi-colored, including many colors that have never been seen in this world before.

Similarly, our hearing will be perfected. Right now we are practically deaf compared to many animals, and we can only hear a small segment of the tremendous spectrum of musical sounds that exist. But what will it be then, when our hearing is completely enlarged to hear all that there is?

What fragrances will we enjoy at that time from flowers unknown here on earth? What fragrances of frankincense, aloes, myrrh, and a thousand others will waft across the celestial breezes of heaven?

What will the society there be like? We know that each of us will have bodies which will have no pain or aches any longer, no stiff joints or weaknesses of limb, and no pang or twinge at night or in the morning. We will be enjoying perfect health! But the society there—what will that be like?

We know that there will be no loneliness there. In this world, sin separates people. Sin causes us to erect barriers to separate ourselves from one another. Sin alienates parents from children, husbands from wives, and neighbors from neighbors. But in that day, all sin will be gone and we will be joined in a heavenly fellowship, or *koinonia,* the like of which we have never known before. Many in this world have never known much besides loneliness; they have never found a heart with whom theirs can resonate. Even in marriage, they have been separate and lonely. But in that day, loneliness will end. There are people who have never known the feeling of being loved or loving. That too will pass away.

Those who have temporarily passed into the next world and who have experienced that Being who is made of light, who is the Light of the world, have said that the love that emanates from Christ is so overwhelming as to be absolutely palpable. It is a love which can be almost felt and touched, something tangible, a love which is completely and totally overwhelming. We shall know that love in that day, and we shall never again be lonely or feel unloved.

And not only shall we know the love of Christ, but the love of others. There will be no rejection or snobbishness there. There will be no fear of rejection, for everyone you meet will respond to you with perfect love. What a fellowship that will be! And there will be no grief or loss in that world. Many have experienced the brokenheartedness of grief, the separation, as they have watched a loved one lowered into the ground. Husbands or wives, beloved children, or parents have gone beyond—and now those who remain walk alone! There is an ache in the soul where once there was laughter. But there shall be no more parting there.

As John described it metaphorically when he was on Patmos and looked out at the angry sea whose waves broke against the barren rocks of that island prison: "And there was no more sea" (Revelation 21:1). He referred to that which divides and separates. The crystal sea will be near the throne of God but there will be no sea of separation there. No depression.

And there will be no gloom. We shall always be filled with joy in that time, for at His right hand there is joy for evermore. And no failure, either, for all of the abilities and talents that God has given us will then be expanded to their uttermost. We will have abilities beyond what we have ever known here. And those things which make life miserable—jealousies and envies and animosities, coldness, aloofness, rejection—all of those will long be forgotten in the glorious fellowship of the society of the Redeemer.

Conversations in Eternity

And what conversations may we have then? We will be able to find out about all of those things that we always wanted to know and had never been able to find out!

What was it really like in paradise in the beginning? Well, you can just walk down the golden street and knock at the door of Adam's house and ask him. Or maybe you would prefer to talk to Eve.

What was it like when God cleft the sea and brought the people of Israel out from under the heavy hand of Pharaoh? Well, Moses lives just across the park. You can go over and talk to him about that or what it was like when he went up Mount Sinai for forty days alone with God.

What was it like when God caused the sun to stand still? Well, only two doors down is Joshua's house, and you can find out from him.

What was baby Jesus really like? What was He like when He was a child? What did He do during those mysterious years before He was thirty? Well, you can ask Mary if you'd like to know. Or, you can even ask Jesus Himself.

What was the crucifixion really like? You can discuss it with the centurion who said, "Truly, this man was the Son of God" (Mark 15:39). Or with that penitent thief who said, "Remember me when thou comest into thy kingdom" (Luke 23:42).

What did the Apostle Paul mean by that inscrutable passage

in one of his epistles that you always wondered about. Well, there he is, sitting on the park bench. Why don't you just sit down and ask him?

What conversations we will have there in heaven!

And what of the employments of the redeemed in paradise? Many people seem to just sort of stumble into the occupations that fill up most of their lives. Some accident, it seems, brings them to what they do. They look back and say, if they had it to do all over again, they would really have preferred to do something different. You really didn't want to sell shoes; you actually wanted to be a violinist, didn't you? Well, this is your chance. You can learn to play the violin like no one has ever played it in this world. (They hardly had time to warm up compared to the time that you are going to have to practice.) And just think of some of the teachers that will be there. Perhaps you want to complete the violin lessons; then you can take up the cello or the clarinet. (I will be glad to help you out there.) As for me, I am going to learn to sing.

What would you like to do? Perhaps you always wanted to be an artist. Yes, you've had to make beds and fix meals when you really would have loved to paint. Well, there might be time for Raphael to help you with that—when he is not too busy redoing his Michael, the archangel, a once-called "masterpiece" but which he sees now is all wrong because he has now met Michael in person. And there will be time now to learn to paint: to master watercolors, oils, sculpturing, drawing, whatever you like—and then move on to something else.

Maybe what you really wanted, deep down in your heart, was to be an actor. (There is a little bit of ham in you that has never really been cultivated.) Well, why not? Just think of what dramas there will be to portray and what time there will be to see them! This is your opportunity. Just think of some of the great actors that you might have an opportunity to meet!

Perhaps you have never had the time to read all of those books on your shelf that you have always wanted to read but never had the time. Well, there will be plenty of time just to sit down and read under a shady tree on the soft grass of paradise and read to your heart's content.

Maybe you would rather write a book. You have said that you have always wanted to do that. Be my guest: Write a dozen, or how about a hundred. There will be lots of people to read them and plenty of time.

Perhaps you are a scientist. Well, imagine the time that you will have to examine the mysteries of God's creation. Or maybe you are one of those who likes to travel. (I've never been one for much travel. I guess I've done too much of it already. But in that day there won't be any aches or pains or long dull trips.) You'll move as fast as your thoughts can take you: from place to place, from planet to planet, you can explore the entire cosmos. My, what wonders God has created! We haven't the faintest idea what they all are even yet. But you will be able to see them, every one, if you would like to do it.

When you get through with your cosmic tour, maybe you would like to get down to a little business. Jesus said that He would make you ruler over ten cities. If that doesn't take care of all of your desires to run something, then I don't know what will. You can exhibit all of your administrative talents at that point.

Meeting Jesus Christ

When you hear the bells toll and the choir anthems rise and swell, and when you see the multitudes coming from all directions in the Holy City to the Temple of God to worship Christ—you will see Him who is the fairest of ten thousand. And your heart will be so filled with ecstasy that worship will be the greatest experience in paradise. You who loved beauty can see the Rose of Sharon. You who are inclined toward mathematics can compute the age of His reign. You who are lawyers can listen to Him who is the Judge of all the earth. You who are doctors can listen to the wisdom of Him who is the

Great Physician. Yes, we will worship Him who has brought us all the way to paradise. There is no end to the activities in heaven, and I am sure that I have not even barely touched the hem of the garment. All of this can be yours only in Jesus Christ.

Some time ago in a newspaper in California, in a letter to the editor, a scientist expressed the fact that if there really is a heaven and a hell then the most intelligent thing that any human being can do is to be sure that he attains to the one and avoids the other. I thought that such a sentiment as that, coming from a scientist, was, indeed, remarkable. Usually their wisdom in spiritual matters seems to be the very opposite of their scientific wisdom. But how true is what he said! The important thing is that we attain to that great bliss which God has prepared.

And how do we attain it? Well, that was the thought that filled the mind of a young sixteen-and-a-half-year-old boy in England over a hundred years ago now: His name was Charles Haddon Spurgeon and he had only one desire in life. Unlike most sixteen-year-olds whose lives and thoughts are usually rather vain and flippant at that time, he only desired to attain eternal life. He went from church to church and listened to preacher after preacher with little or no help at all. Finally, one cold winter day amidst the snows, he made his way rather dejectedly into a tiny church where only fifteen people were present. Indeed, the snow had kept most people away. I am sure that the preacher that day thought that it was a great disaster for the kingdom of God in that little community. Although most people had stayed home from worship, nevertheless the minister began to preach his sermon on the text: "Look unto me, and be ye saved, all the ends of the earth; for I am God, and there is none else" (Isaiah 45:22).

Young Spurgeon, with an anxious and almost despairing look on his face, listened to the message and tried to piece together what was being said. He tried to understand how he could have eternal life. But he was having very little success, and obviously the expression of his countenance revealed that fact.

Finally, right in the middle of the sermon, the minister stopped his preaching, fixed his eyes upon the young man, and, pointing at him, spoke to him personally, saying, "Young man, you are miserable."

Spurgeon could not argue the point. He had never had a preacher stop his sermon and point right at him and speak to him personally. He sat upright in his seat. The preacher continued, "And you will stay miserable forever unless you heed my text: 'Look unto me, and be ye saved, all the ends of the earth; for I am God, and there is none else.' "

Young Charles Spurgeon lifted up his eyes to the cross, the cross of Calvary where Christ died for his sins. If the preacher had told him to do something, he would have done anything. If he had said that for fifty lashes with a cat-o-nine-tails he could have eternal life, he would have instantly bared his back to receive the blows. But he simply said, "Look," "look"—not "do," not "accomplish," not "attain"—but the least that anyone could do, to simply look.

Spurgeon looked unto Jesus, a look of faith, and he put his trust in the Savior. Charles Haddon Spurgeon was converted that dismal, snowy day in England, that day of failure at that little church.

But tens of thousands, nay, tens of millions of people have since heard or read the words of Charles Spurgeon, the greatest preacher that ever lived. And those words spread out all over the world, not only in England and Europe and America, but all the way to the islands of the sea and Australia. People eagerly waited for the weekly messages of the great preacher of London.

My friends, I would say to you today: I hope that your heart yearns for that water of life, for that life everlasting. I would urge you now the same way to look to Christ, to place your trust in Him. "The gift of God is eternal life through Jesus

Christ, our Lord" (Romans 6:23). The most wonderful thing that I can say about all I have told you is that the paradisical joy which Christ has prepared is yours free. It was paid for at infinite cost by Christ, but it is offered gratuitously, freely, graciously, unto you. It can be yours by faith if you simply reach out with the hand of a beggar—to accept the great gift of a king. Do you have that gift of life eternal? Do you know assuredly that you are on your way to heaven? If not, you have missed out on the greatest thing that can be known in this world, that blessed assurance that Jesus is yours—that foretaste of glory divine. And you *will* miss out on the joys everlasting, the glory of paradise unless you heed that text and receive that gift today.

"I believe in the life everlasting." Yes, but even more glorious is the fact that I *know* that it is mine. Do you?